PRAISE FOR
Your Writing Matters

"This is a book of welcome—which means that it's a book of openings, the kind of openings that every writer needs to be inspired and connected—to the world, to themselves, to their fellow writers, to their stories ... and to all of the mysteries that touch us as creators.

"'You deserve to create what's in you to create,' writes Keiko O'Leary. Yes. This book radiates yes. It radiates awakening."

> —Grant Faulkner, Executive Director of National Novel Writing Month

"A beautifully written meditation on the writer's life. The minute I started reading this, I thought, 'Oh, I'm home!' This book speaks to the writer in me, not the published person in me. I can't speak highly enough about this book."

> —Julie A. Fast, bestselling author of *Getting it Done When You're Depressed*

"If you want to write but feel intimidated, or you start writing but get discouraged, or even if you already write a lot but would like some encouragement and celebration—this book is for you."

> —C. Borst, author of *Soldiers in Grey*

"Keiko's book inspired me to start working on a novel that I had been wanting to write." —Erin Garcia, author, educator

"A reassuring mix of encouragement and practical advice."

—Aidan Doyle, author of *The Writer's Book of Doubt*

"Keiko O'Leary doesn't just love reading and writing. She is *in love* with reading and writing, and in love with readers and writers. Page after page, we come to realize we're not odd or alone. She believes in you and me unconditionally.

"Writers like us are connected through what we read and write and create. Writing and creating are, in fact, our life-sustaining provisions. 'Claim your peers.' It will free you up to write, to heal, to memorialize, and to speak out."

—Lorraine Haataia, Ph.D., founder of Prolific Writers Life

"This book stirred me deeply. [It's] a book that welcomed me, non-judgmentally, back home to writing. Your Writing Matters is unconditional love. And wisdom. Keiko O'Leary's voice is an unpretentious beckoning to never give up—not on our writing, not on ourselves."

—Ruth Littmann-Ashkenazi, author, photographer

"Insightful and interesting."

—Katy Morgan, author of the Compound Series

Your Writing Matters

Your Writing Matters

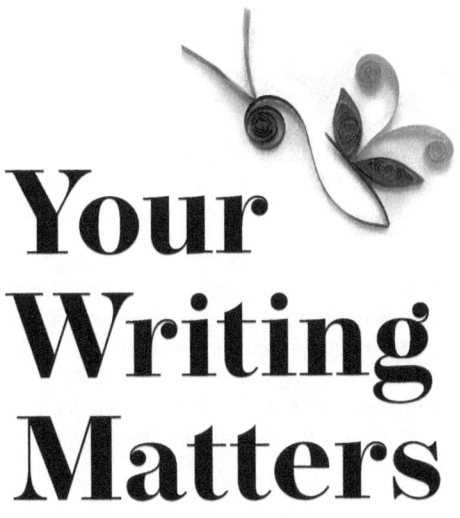

34 QUICK ESSAYS TO GET UNSTUCK
AND STAY INSPIRED

KEIKO O'LEARY

Thinking Ink Press
Campbell, California

YOUR WRITING MATTERS. Copyright © 2022 by Keiko O'Leary.

Some of the contents of this book appeared originally in slightly or significantly different form on *www.WriteToTheEnd.com*, the literary journal *My Kitchen Table*, and *www.KeikoOLeary.com*.

All rights reserved. No part of this book may be reproduced or transmitted in any form or by any means, electronic or mechanical, including photocopying and recording, or introduced into any information storage and retrieval system without the written permission of the copyright owner and the publisher of this book. Brief quotations may be used in reviews. For more information, contact *editorial@thinkinginkpress.com*.

Published by Thinking Ink Press
P.O. Box 1411
Campbell, California 95009
www.ThinkingInkPress.com
First edition, 2022

Paperback ISBN 978-1-942480-34-1
Ebook ISBN 978-1-942480-35-8

Project Credits
Editor: Liza Olmsted
Copy Editor: Marilyn Horn
Interior Book Designer: Betsy Miller

Typefaces used in this book: Azo Sans, Georgia, Operetta 12.

Dedication

To my husband, Sergio Etcheverry, who once upon a time said, "Keiko, why don't you stop trying to turn your friends into writers and go make friends with some writers?"

And in memory of Jan Petrucha, whose great love for this world reminds me to be brave and write.

CONTENTS

Introduction: Writers Are a Family 11

We Welcome All Writing 14

Give the Gift of Unconditional Love: Write 21

Please Finish Your Story 24

Your Subconscious Is Trying to Help You 29

What Is Fiction For? 32

You Don't Have to Be Special,
You Just Have to Stick Around 35

Writing Practice: A Method You Can Try 39

My New Writing Coach 41

Watson Loves Me 45

Why Write to the End? 49

Claim Your Peers 54

Keep a Compliments List 58

The Real Life of Fiction 65

The Parable of Don McLean *or*
Why Encourage Everyone, Including Yourself 69

Get Results Faster by Using Bright Spots 73

Don't Show Your Work to Your Friends 77

You Can Never Say Thank You 80

The Serving Dinner Model of Publishing 84

The Greeks Don't Own the Stars 89

You're Probably More Qualified Than You Feel 94

No *Enterprise* 101

How to Believe in Yourself 105

Writing People Off 108

Colorless Green Ideas Crashed My Car *or*
Your Right to Say Things That Don't Make Sense 111

(The Cure For) Fiction Deficiency Syndrome 115

Accept the Magic of Imagination 117

"I Want These but Don't Know How" 122

Borges Loves Me? 126

Do It More 135

Coming Out About Obsession 137

Only *Enterprise* 139

Be Brave and Write 143

Not the End 145

Recommended Reading 147

Acknowledgements 149

INTRODUCTION: WRITERS ARE A FAMILY

Your writing can make a difference. Through your writing, you help people experience meaning, not only in what you write, but also in their own lives.

My wish for you is to develop a true and living relationship with your writing. For you to accept yourself as a writer. For you to find community with other writers. For you to share your work, and know that it matters. For you to know that in this beautiful, meaningful endeavor of writing, you are not alone, and you are welcome. I made this book so that when you doubt those things, you have someone who will help you get back to believing in them.

While I was working on this book, I got a chance to go to the O'Leary Family Picnic for the first time since before my kids were born. So much more than a family reunion, the picnic defines and celebrates what it means to be an O'Leary.

The picnic happens in Montana, and though no one has ever treated me badly in Montana, when I was a kid the state was not exactly a model of ethnic diversity. Back then, my sister and I were (as I recall) the only nonwhite people at the picnic.* In fact, some of our cousins called us "the brown cousins," but only because our skin was brown compared to theirs, not because they thought anything of it.

At home in diverse California, we were constantly being asked "What are you?" and having to explain that we were "half Japanese." But at the picnic, we were never treated as "half O'Leary." We were 100% O'Leary, just like everyone else. Nowadays there are O'Learys of many races at the picnic, with different percentages of "O'Leary blood," but everyone is welcomed as a full member of the family, because that is what we are.

At my writing group, I insist upon welcome. Everyone must be welcomed, even people I don't get along with personally, because we are all writers. We are all part of a family, and that is more important than anything else.

Even if you haven't written for a long time; even if you're just dreaming about writing and haven't started yet; no matter what you're saying to yourself about how you could never belong or be good enough or whatever, if you're reading this book, I'll bet you're a writer. Maybe you're not confident enough to call yourself that yet, but look into your heart. Do you see the desire to write?

---

* I guess my mom was also nonwhite, but seriously, who has that kind of insight about their mom?

You can trust that desire as the sign that you are part of this family. You need never doubt your belonging again. Instead, do as our family does: write.

We are waiting to hear your words.

Welcome home.

How to Use This Book

Each of these essays is complete in itself. You can open the book anywhere and start reading. I often use that method for books of advice, and it is amazing how often I find just what I need. Many of the essays mention topics that others treat more fully. I've included footnotes to let you know when another essay relates—you could use them to decide what to read next. And of course you could always read them in order.

Some of the essays suggest specific things you can do, and I hope you do them, because concrete action will take you far. But it's not enough. We need somebody to elevate our experience, to show us why our actions matter. We need somebody to tell us a story, or give us a poem, or make some kind of art that shows us the meaning of our lives and of our work. That's what writers do, and that's what I've tried to do for you.

How to Pronounce My Name

Keiko is a Japanese name. If you speak English, you can think of the word *cake* and say CAKE-oh.

WE WELCOME ALL WRITING

At my writing group, Write to the End, we do two main activities: we write, and we welcome all writing. These two activities are the foundation of our group. Let's pretend you've just come to the group for the first time, and I'll show you how it works.

Welcome. I welcome you, and I welcome your writing: all of your writing, not just the parts you think are worth welcoming.

This is Anthony, and this is Betsy, and Liza, and Gayle, and David. That's enough names for now. You'll get to know everyone as we go along. But just know that we are all here to support each other as writers.

Let's Write!

If you're willing, we can have a writing session together right now. Just set a timer for 20 minutes and write continuously until the timer goes off. Or do whatever writing process you prefer for an amount of time that you choose. If you've never written before, or if you're busy right now, you could try five minutes, or even one minute. If no timer is at hand, you could fill up a page or the back of an envelope or a screen on your phone.

I bet you're still reading, thinking you'll do it later.* I do that too, and it's totally fine to just keep reading. At the same time, you chose this book because you want to write, so I'd better encourage you at least a little bit. This is a great opportunity to do what you want to do, and it only has to take a minute. Plus, think of all your fellow writers, who we're pretending are here for this pretend writing group session. We're all here supporting each other by writing together.

One last note: if you're planning to stop reading until you can do the writing session later, hey, you don't even want to know how many books I've abandoned in a swamp of guilt because of a plan like that. I don't want that to happen when we've only known each other for a few paragraphs. Let's just agree that you'll write later and keep reading now, okay?

So, if it works for you, go ahead and do a writing session right now, and come back when you're finished.

Ready to write? Go!

॰

---

* But if you already did a writing session, hooray! You'll fit right in at Write to the End.

Welcome back. If you didn't do it, no worries. You can have a writing session soon. For now, go ahead and keep reading.

How to Welcome All Writing

Now we've come to the part where we practice welcoming all writing. At the group, we read our work aloud and listen to each other.

Imagine yourself at Write to the End. People have just written whatever they've written, from disconnected notes to scenes of novels, from sonnets to to-do lists. And now we are going around the table, reading these things out loud: what everyone just wrote, during the previous 20 minutes. And we all turn off our expectations and listen; we take it in without context; we don't require it to be anything other than what it is.

It's hardest to do it for yourself, for your own writing, but I'm inviting you to give it a try.

Now it's your turn to read. We are all listening, without judgement. It would be great if you actually read your words out loud. Of course you don't have to, but how about you at least read them over silently, and when you do, try this:

Turn off everything. Be blank. Be nothing, and become what you read. Let what you read be all there is in that moment.

The way to keep writing is to welcome all writing. Therefore, the way to be a writer is to welcome all writing.

Turn off your judgement and smartness, your desire for something to be a certain way, your hopes of greatness or fears of awfulness. Turn off all your expectations, and see what you wrote for what it actually is. Pretend someone else wrote it, and let it affect you the way *it* wants to. Let yourself be defenseless against it. This can be hard or scary, but it can also be exhilarating.

As you do this, the group will support you. It really will, even though we are only pretend. If you start to crack or even break, the structure of the group will hold you. And most likely, what you've written will become the glue that sticks the pieces back together stronger than before, and you will be a better writer for it.

Go ahead. Read your work, and welcome it for what it is. We are all listening and welcoming it, too.

༄

Thanks for trying that. I welcome what you wrote.

If you didn't do it, you can always try it another time.

It's important to say that I don't want you to suspend judgement forever. When your evaluative self comes back, if you don't like what you wrote, that's okay. You are free to abandon it or revise it, and you'll get the chance to write something else very soon.

If we were really at Write to the End, we'd write and read two more times before the end of the meeting. Feel free to do two more sessions if you'd like. Set a timer, write, read what you wrote and welcome it. We'll be here to support you. (And if you aren't going to do them right now, go ahead and keep reading. You'll write again soon.)

◈

So now you've experienced Write to the End. Yay! Come back any time.

Why We Welcome All Writing

Have you ever written something really good and then not written anything for weeks on end? Probably that was because you wanted the next thing to be just as good. This is a common cause of writer's block.

The best cure I know is to practice welcoming all writing.

If you welcome all writing, you'll be willing to write, because you'll know it's okay if this time you don't like what you wrote. You'll be able to keep writing over time, because you'll focus on doing the physical act of writing rather than on your opinion of its results. You'll tolerate disappointment because writing—not recognition or judgement—will be the foundation of your writing life. Writing something "good" is never guaranteed, so it makes a bad foundation. Instead, every time you write, be glad that you are writing, and welcome whatever comes.

I'm not saying to publish first drafts; I'm not saying you need to like what you wrote. People do sometimes create great pieces in these writing group sessions, but that's not the purpose of the sessions. The purpose is to cultivate writers. The purpose is to keep us writing and improving and deepening our relationships with our own work and with the place all writing comes from.

You want to be a writer. Writers write. The way to keep writing is to welcome all writing. Therefore, the way to be a writer is to welcome all writing.

My goal is to cultivate writers, so I welcome all writing. You are a writer, and I welcome you.

GIVE THE GIFT OF
UNCONDITIONAL LOVE: WRITE

I'm a visual artist as well as a writer, and I opened up *1984* the other day, with the intention of looking for details for a painting I wanted to do. I meant only to skim a few paragraphs, get an idea of what London is supposed to look like, and then get back to planning the painting. But I couldn't keep my focus on the research. Without realizing I was doing it, I started to *read*. Because *1984* is just that beautiful, that compelling, that—home? Is that what it feels like: coming home? I'm generally a nervous and lonely person, always second-guessing the loving intentions of friends and even family, always trying to hide my true self because I'm sure I will be rejected. But reading *1984*, I become unselfconscious. Reading *1984*, I am completely myself, and I have no thought that I might not be accepted that way. For me, the experience of reading *1984* is an experience of being loved unconditionally.

And you know what? Once upon a time, *1984* didn't exist. Once upon a time, George Orwell wrote and struggled and edited and wrote and threw away whole paragraphs and rewrote and gave up and kept going anyway, in order to create that book. In order to create a text that gives me the experience of unconditional love. Maybe you hate *1984*, but I'll bet you've read something that gave you that experience, too. And maybe, if you don't quit, if you work hard to master your craft and give your pieces form and get them into the world, something you write will give someone else that experience.

As humans we always seem to expect something in return: maybe we can't truly love another person unconditionally. But our writing can. So keep working. I'm cheering for you.

As humans we always seem to expect something in return: maybe we can't truly love another person unconditionally. But our writing can.

PLEASE FINISH YOUR STORY

Remember that story you started last week? (Or maybe it was last month, or a few years ago.) I want to read the whole thing. In fact, I want to purchase a publication that contains it and read the published version. But you haven't finished it, have you?

That's okay: I haven't finished a whole bunch of my stories either. It's the nature of creative work to start more things than we finish. And it's not that I want to force you to finish a story you don't want to finish, a story that's not for you. Or even a story that was for you at one time but is now so far in the past that you couldn't write it anymore even if you wanted to. But the ones that are still "on" for you, please finish those. Because your readers are waiting for them.

What Do You Mean, "Readers"?

If we're still pretending you're a member of our writing group, then Betsy and Anthony and Ruth and the rest of us at Write to the End are your readers. But even if it's just you, this is your internal reader's experience—not writer-you, but reader-you, the one who reads what you've written. There might even be multiple reader-yous: for example, your 9-year-old self who always wanted a story like the one you've started.

Your Readers' Experience

We, your readers, hear part of your story, maybe the part you wrote in 20 minutes while sitting around a table with us at Write to the End. We get excited about it. We get interested in the characters. We want to see what will happen to them. We want to know why certain details of the story are the way they are, because they seem important. If the text you've written were printed in a book, we would keep reading past our bedtime in order to find out these things. An external reader might feel this way about anything you write. And when you write a story you are excited about, your internal reader feels this way.

Then the next time you write, or the next week at the writing group, or even just randomly as we go about our days, your readers are hoping to hear the next part of the story. I know that stories don't always come out linearly; I know you can't promise the next installment as though this were a serial on TV. But we still want it. The brain science people would say our biology expects it. This is why people keep bugging you to work on something.

Life is short, and you're the only one who can make the work that matters to you.

But as a writer, you can't just write what other people want. Your first responsibility is to your internal reader: it's important to notice your own interest in a story.

Don't Finish a Story You Don't Care About

I once wrote a very short story called "The Death of the Station Wagon," in which some linguistics students hear a loud noise, look for the source, and discover that their professor's station wagon has died. That's the whole plot. People asked me to write more; they thought it was an interesting beginning and wondered what happened next. But I'm not going to try to find out what happens next, because I think that story is either complete or failed. If I ever work on that story again, I might add a second thread to try to make the events more meaningful, but the sequence of events is already complete: after the station wagon dies, the story is over. So if you wanted to hear what happens next, I'm sorry. Nothing happens next. That universe ceases to exist.

I'm not asking you to keep working on a story you know has no future, one your internal reader doesn't care about, or one you think is done. Don't let an external reader persuade you to do that, no matter how interested they are in the story. They can write their own story.

Life is short, and you're the only one who can make the work that matters to you. Say no to narratives you don't care about.

Finish the Ones You Care About

I'm done with "The Death of the Station Wagon." But I'm still interested in my unfinished story "Dazzlewelts," about a woman who starts cheating on her fiancé with someone she meets in a dream. My readers wish I would finish that one, and I do too, because I want to see how it turns out.

You have stories like that. Please finish them. I want to read them. Your internal reader does, too.

YOUR SUBCONSCIOUS IS TRYING TO HELP YOU

Do you ever get a phrase in your head, maybe a line from a poem you learned as a kid? Or it could be the title of a story, or a bit of dialogue, or even a few words from your own work. Or sometimes a song that you haven't heard in years, but now you can't get it out of your head.

Probably you don't do anything with these phrases, except maybe complain about the song.

But what if these phrases are messages?

When my grandma was dying, I got a line from a Paul Simon song in my head: "the rose of Jericho and the bougainvillea." I hadn't heard the song in years, and I decided to listen to the entire album (*The Rhythm of the Saints*, a brilliant collection of music and poetry). It gave me perspective on the way my grandma had influenced our family's life and my life, and I felt like I understood her story better. And when I finally got to the actual line, it turned out to be in a passage about a funeral. That was the first time in the grieving process that I was able to cry.

I know that art helps us grieve and celebrate, that it helps us experience and make sense of our feelings, that it helps us live and choose how to live. But I hadn't realized that the art I need has often come to me through seemingly random phrases that popped up in my mind. Every time I go listen to a song that's stuck in my head, I find what I need at that moment. And it doesn't just work with songs. Sometimes a title will float through my mind ("We Will Drink a Fish Together" by Bill Johnson), or a line of a poem ("What immortal hand or eye" from "The Tyger" by William Blake), and if I go to the source and let myself experience the entire piece, it is always what I need. Sometimes it's not what I want: sometimes I don't feel ready for the transformation that the art brings me. But I have chosen to live as a protagonist, and that means I must suffer change in order to experience meaning.

Looking back on all the times this has worked, I conclude that something is trying to help me. Let's say it's my subconscious mind. Whatever it is, it's sending me messages of art that can change me in the way I need to be changed.

It sometimes even uses my own writing. While I was editing this book, I experienced great swaths of zero motivation. Sometimes the only thing that kept me going was rereading the essays and trying to take my own advice. And plenty of times, what led me to the essay that helped was a little phrase that floated into my head, seemingly out of nowhere. But now I think it's not out of nowhere: it's out of somewhere that knows what I'm going through and is trying to help.

You might not live in a sea of allusions like I do, but still, if a phrase pops into your head, maybe try tracking down and experiencing the entire work. It could be just what you need.

P.S. These phrases can also help you solve problems in your writing. If you're stuck on something in a piece you're working on, listen for the phrases that pop into your head. They could lead you to a solution.

WHAT IS FICTION FOR?

During one of the most stressful times in my life, I spent a couple of hours every day reading Philip K. Dick novels. I did this for three or four months. Novels such as *Martian Time-Slip* and *Flow My Tears, the Policeman Said* allowed me to spend time being insane, and I think that helped me be sane the rest of the time. I suppose this would be classified as "escape," which is one of the uses of fiction that people often cite. I think of it more as "medicine" or "treatment," but I guess I can accept "escape." This is the only time I can think of that I've used fiction for something resembling escape.

My main use of fiction is the opposite of escape. It's to wake up, to be here, to open myself to the wonder and beauty of life and this world. A story like Lawrence Watt-Evans's "Why I Left Harry's All-Night Hamburgers" produces this effect and is also about it at the same time.

Another way I use fiction is to know what matters and to have an example of how to live. Janet Kagan's "The Nutcracker Coup" shows me how to keep standing as myself in the face of hate. I read this story before I was much interested in "real life," but later I also found the same strong and beautiful truth in the story of Rosa Parks's "no" and the Montgomery Bus Boycott. Fiction shows me how to live as my best self, to do what's right, for all of us, even when it's not what's easy.

I also use fiction as a source of human relationships. I read Albert Camus' *The Plague* to hang out with people whose company I enjoy; I read Sherlock Holmes to participate in the friendship I have with the narrator.* Reading *1984*, I experience unconditional love, something uncommon in nonfictional human relationships.** What about Orson Scott Card's *Ender's Game*? My original use of this book was as an initiatory experience, a rite of passage. But I reread it for many of the uses I've already mentioned. Most of the stories I love serve more than one of these uses, maybe all of them.

A final use of fiction is something that can come from any writing: a pure sensual experience. I read Julio Cortázar for his stories, but also for his language, to be flowed along by words, to be treated by a sentence as though it were a lover. I read Cortázar in Spanish, and sometimes I don't know half the words, but I still enjoy it. Maybe enjoyment is the overarching use of fiction. Could

---

* See "Watson Loves Me" on page 45.

** See "Give the Gift of Unconditional Love: Write" on page 21.

that possibly be true? Could the world really be as loving as that? I will have to think about this and get back to you.

For now, it's your turn. What do you use fiction for?

YOU DON'T HAVE TO BE SPECIAL, YOU JUST HAVE TO STICK AROUND

I always think the authors I love are magic, that they are somehow different from me, and that's why they are successful (famous, published, whatever). But that's not true.

What does Galway Kinnell have that you don't have? What does Mary Oliver have? Nothing! (Or nothing that you can do anything about.) The only difference is that they kept at it. For years. And years. You can't control things you can't control, like luck or inborn talent (if there is such a thing). But here are three practices that you *can* control. They will make a difference:

- **Practice Persistence**—keep going! Usually this means taking some sort of action: writing, revising. Some days it might seem like you're not going anywhere, but even if you've lost all hope and can't take any action today, if you say to yourself, "I'm still here," that's persistence.

You deserve to create what's in you to create.

- **Build Skill**—most of what people think of as talent is actually skill. If you want to get good at something, you can.* All you have to do is study. My definition of study has three parts:
    1. find people who are good at what you want to do,
    2. see what they do to get better, and
    3. do that.

- **Seek Community**—connect with people in your field. Meet other writers, editors, anyone who does something related to what you do. Write charming notes to authors you admire.** Go to events. Make your own events. Join organizations. Make friends with people who understand what you're trying to do and who want to help you succeed.

The reason community is so important is that it helps you do the other practices. Keep going? Much easier if your friends are doing it too. Improve your skills? Hey, let's take a class *together*. Humans are social animals. Other people are a huge biological influence on your behavior. You can

---

* Please read Daniel Coyle's *The Talent Code: Greatness Isn't Born. It's Grown. Here's How*.

** For more about charming notes, read Carolyn See's *Making a Literary Life*.

use that to your advantage instead of letting it bring you down.

There's a fourth practice that you probably need. It's totally fine to write just for yourself, and that's enough for many people. But if you're reading this, it's probably not enough for you. If writing is your art, you need to release your work. The pile-up-great-work-in-a-drawer method pretty much only ever worked for Emily Dickinson (and, by the way, she actually did submit her poems). You don't have to show people right away; you don't have to show everything; and you definitely don't have to show it to everyone.[*] But the basic message is this: do the above three things, and be willing to let your work make its way into the world by whatever means makes sense at the time, and you give your work its best chance to make a difference.

You deserve to create what's in you to create.

So please, stick around. Control the things you can control: keep going, improve your skills, seek out community, and release your work. Give yourself the chance to succeed.

---

[*] See "Don't Show Your Work to Your Friends" on page 77.

WRITING PRACTICE: A METHOD YOU CAN TRY

Often when I write, I use Natalie Goldberg's method of writing practice.* Basically, you set a timer, and then you write without stopping or thinking until the timer goes off. The goal is to write down first thoughts. Goldberg explains first thoughts as "the way the mind first flashes on something." Writing practice is a form of welcoming your writing. When you want to write, it's easy to wait for a "good idea." You end up rejecting thought after thought in the quest for one that's "good enough." Writing practice is the opposite of that. It's not *wait for a good idea* but

---

* You can find Natalie Goldberg's rules for writing practice all over the internet, but I invite you to read her books. *Wild Mind: Living the Writer's Life* was my first introduction to writing practice, and it is probably more helpful for prose writers. Her most famous book is *Writing Down the Bones: Freeing the Writer Within*. It is also a wonderful introduction to writing practice, and is probably more helpful for poets. She has many other books that I love, but those are good to start with.

rather *accept what you have already flashed on, even if it doesn't make sense.* When you welcome first thoughts, you'll notice more first thoughts. When you welcome the tip of a thread of a piece of writing, the thread lets you pull it, and more of the piece comes through. It's scary to do, but don't stop, don't close off. I'm scared, too. I close off sometimes, too. But I'm always trying to improve my skill of staying open, welcoming first thoughts, and allowing the thoughts to come through. (I am calling them thoughts, but they come in many forms: visions, images, words, sensations.)

The good thing about writing practice is that all you have to do is "keep your hand moving" and do your best to write down first thoughts. You don't have to do anything with these thoughts later. You can choose what you turn into a piece; you can choose how you edit and what you publish. But if you welcome first thoughts and write them down, you'll have something to choose from.

MY NEW WRITING COACH

I'm going to be my own writing coach. I will read my first draft of the story I'm working on, and I'll say to myself, "Hey, Keiko, this is really good! Keep working on it!"

I will reply, "Really?"

"Yes!" I'll say. I'll be so enthusiastic I will convince myself. I will say, "Write a second draft. I want to see it."

"Okay," I'll say. And I'll send myself the next draft.

When I get it, I'll call myself up right away. "Okay," I'll tell myself, "This is really starting to turn into something."

"Thank you," I'll say. "But I don't know where to go next. Do you think you could …?"

"Sure." I'll sound very encouraging. I will help myself learn to figure things out for myself. "What do you think is missing?" I'll ask.

"Well," I'll say, "I think I need to know more about what the houses were like in San Francisco at the turn of the century. And how much they're still like that today." I'll think for a minute. I won't interrupt myself. "You know," I'll say, "I'd really like to have it set in a real house, one that's actually there. I love it when people do that."

"I've noticed that in your work, too," I'll say.

I will be impressed and flattered at first, but then I'll sigh. "I never seem to manage to do the research."

I know what it's like to feel defeated like that. But I will have the solution. "You know," I'll tell myself, "research is just an excuse to read things you're interested in."

"I guess so."

"Go to the library. Find some books."

"Well …" I will hesitate. I won't believe I deserve it.

"Go ahead. I want to see the third draft, the one with the details set."

"All right," I'll say. And I'll go to the library. I'll write the third draft. I'll send it to myself.

"I think you should send this around for a beta read," I'll tell myself. "It's time for some peer critique."

"I want to fix a few things still …" I'll say.

"No, remember what Gayle said: Do beta on things that aren't quite ready. Hey, I'm sure Ruth will love this one. And she'll probably be able to help you even out the facts, like she did with 'Willie Blake.' And Anthony might know specifics of that neighborhood even, or the time period."

"Well—" I'll say.

"And Liza is a historian, and Betsy—"

"All right."

"Are you typing the email?"

"Yes."

I'll stay on the phone with myself until I've sent it.

When I get the beta comments back, I'll go over to my house and sit with myself to go over them. Or better yet, I'll meet myself for coffee. I'll help myself understand what the comments mean for my story. I'll draw out of myself what the story wants to be. I'll help myself excavate the fossil. I'll buy myself another latte and make sure I leave with a plan for the next draft.

When I send myself the next draft, I'll reply, "Submit this." When I balk, I'll tell myself to send it to the Flash Fiction Forum.* "That will be less scary," I'll say. "You know them. And it's not publication, it's just a reading." I'll agree. I'll call myself up and stay on the phone with myself while I submit it. Later, when it gets accepted, I'll call myself to say congratulations.

Of course I'll go to the Forum to see myself read. I'll introduce myself to my writing friends. When it's time for me to read onstage, I'll sit in the audience and listen. After I'm done reading, I'll tell myself I did a great job. I'll make sure I write down any compliments in my compliments list.** I'll also make a note of any comments the audience members give me so that I can see if they need to be

---

* The Flash Fiction Forum is a curated live event in San José, California. It features authors reading their short pieces, including flash fiction, poetry, and more.

** See "Keep a Compliments List" on page 58.

incorporated, but I'll tell myself to wait and not think about it yet. "Just enjoy the rest of the Forum," I'll say.

The next day, I will get together with myself and help myself do the final draft. We'll choose the first place where I'll submit it. I'll stay with myself until I've mailed it off, and then I'll take myself out for lunch.

WATSON LOVES ME

Dr. Watson loves me. I know because he treats me kindly, explains things clearly, never sends a harsh word in my direction. I know because he's willing to be vulnerable, to take me into his confidence. He is a gentleman narrator; he is warm and welcoming; he expresses his love through the care he takes in his sentences.

But I also know he loves me because he loves Holmes.

Sherlock Holmes is a hard person to love. He hasn't succeeded at making a lasting friendship with anyone except Watson. He never seems to be able to express or possibly even feel regular human emotions.

But Watson loves Holmes anyway, cares for him, treats him with loyalty and respect and warmth and friendship, even if Holmes doesn't feel like he deserves it. And because this is fiction, everything Watson does for Holmes, he does for me, the reader. I am similar to Holmes in many negative ways: I am unstable and obsessive; I overvalue my work; I'm awkward in social situations. I often feel like I don't deserve friendship because of these things, but when

I see Watson loving Holmes in spite of those same traits, I realize that I am lovable even with those traits. That's the magic of fiction.

When I am lonely or sad, when I need a kind hand on my shoulder, I turn to Watson. The Sherlock Holmes stories are often repetitive in their structure, with pages of summary, not much plot, and barely a character arc to speak of. I almost never read them anymore to find out what happens or to solve the mystery. I read them to spend time with Watson, to participate in a living relationship between narrator and reader, a relationship that is no less real than Holmes and Watson's celebrated friendship, and no less real than a relationship between two nonfictional humans.

Why am I saying this? To tell you to write? Of course, yes! Write! Maybe you will write a character who becomes your reader's true friend, or maybe you will write a story that lets your reader experience unconditional love.* But I think there's something else here, too.

There are many types of narrators, and they show us different ways we can be. Chuck Palahniuk's narrator in *Survivor* hates the reader and shows it. Borges's self-narrator in "The Aleph" is so journalistic that none of his emotions reach the reader at all. Walt Whitman's narrator in *Leaves of Grass* makes love to the universe in a way

---

* See "Give the Gift of Unconditional Love: Write" on page 21.

When I ask the question "How shall I live?" I always look to literature for the answer.

that is practically obscene. These people show us different ways to tell a story, but they also show us different ways to live. Maybe I will never allow myself to be as exuberant as Whitman, but he shows me that it's okay to *feel* exuberant. A first-person narrator expands our idea of human experience. It lets us see more ways of being human; it lets us accept parts of ourselves we might otherwise deny.

As a reader, I identify with the negative qualities of Holmes, and I therefore receive healing through Watson's friendship. But I also get to see what it's like to be Watson, and I have a chance to identify with him, too. I have a chance to believe in the part of myself that can be a true friend and show it without hesitation.

When I ask the question "How shall I live?" I always look to literature for the answer. Watson has shown me his answer, and that helps me find my own.

Author's Note: Since I originally wrote this essay, I started keeping a compliments list and working on impostor syndrome.* I've come to feel my worthiness more and more often, and I live so much more in the place that Watson has shown me.

---

* See "Keep a Compliments List" on page 58.

WHY WRITE TO THE END?

My writing group has been together for quite a while (I started running the group in 2004, and some of our members have been with us since then), but it took us over seven years to find a name. Why did it take so long? I don't know. Maybe it had something to do with wanting the name to reflect our identity as a group. Why did we choose the name Write to the End? That's easy: it's the advice we most often give each other.

Often new members come to the group and ask for feedback on their as-yet-uncompleted novel. Or someone who's been with us a while will get an idea for a story, write a few scenes of it during the writing sessions, and then ask everybody what we think. This seems perfectly reasonable on the surface, and is, I think, why many people start going to writing groups in the first place.

However, as a group we have learned that giving feedback on the actual writing is not helpful in these situations. Early in the creation of a piece, your understanding of it is fragile. Feedback can take you off track. You can waste a lot of time making changes, only to discover later that the changes don't match the piece. Worse, you could get discouraged and abandon the piece altogether.

When you know the shape of your whole piece, its purpose, its theme, the effect it's trying to create, that helps you decide the experience you want to lead the reader through. Every decision becomes easier once you find the unifying principle of your piece. But often you can't discover it until you know the shape of the whole piece, especially since the ending is often a surprise. (If you use an outline, this advice applies to reaching the end of your outline.) The purpose of getting to *The End* isn't the end itself, but rather that getting there helps you discover the unifying principle.

What we invariably say to people when they ask for feedback is, "Have you gotten to The End yet? Have you finished the first draft?" And if the answer is no, then our feedback is "Keep going! Get to The End! When you get there, you'll be able to answer your own question."

There are quite a few variations on this advice. For example,

Writer: I've just realized I need Character X to be an insurance salesman instead of a knight, and the book needs to start off in Palm Springs two years earlier!

Group: Write yourself a note to that effect, pretend you already made all those changes and they are wonderful, and KEEP GOING! Get to The End!

Finish what you start instead of worrying about what you've written.

Or

Writer: Do you think I should structure this story as a series of flashbacks, or would it make more sense to do it in chronological order?

Group: Finish the story however you can. When you reach The End, then you'll be able to figure out what story you're actually telling and whether it will work better told in flashbacks or chronologically. Don't waste time deciding that now. Just KEEP GOING! Get to The End!

Or

Writer: Should I use first or third person? Past or present tense? I keep switching as I write.

Group: Use whatever gets the story out. Switch all you want—that's easy to fix later. Anything that helps you get the story out is the right thing for that moment. KEEP GOING! Get to The End!

These examples are from writing narrative, but I've used the general principle for all types of writing, from poetry to essays to how-to articles and even email.

In my writing group's search for a name, we tried many alternatives. But as soon as we thought of the name Write to the End, we knew it was a good one for our group. And we're also experiencing an unexpected benefit: it's very satisfying and motivating for the name of our group to be a sort of rallying cry. When one of us is getting bogged down in our writing, another of us can say, "It's going to be okay. Just write to *The End!*" I think it has made our group stronger and is helping our members with their writing projects.

Of course "Write to the End" has other meanings too, which as writers we appreciate and use.[*] But its most useful meaning is to finish what you start instead of worrying about what you've written. If you're looking for advice for your writing project, you might try writing to *The End*.

---

[*] For example, "Write for your whole life."

CLAIM YOUR PEERS

Do you sometimes feel like you don't belong, or that you're not up to the level of people you admire?

A while back, I started going to a new poetry class, and when I first saw the poems people had sent for critique, I was afraid I would be out of my depth. These people were serious poets. They had a very high skill level. Upon a first reading, I did not have anything I could say that would improve their poems. I had to read each poem multiple times, study it, look for its structure, really work to see what the poet was doing. Wow, these people were good. Would they even find my contribution worth looking at?

But the first night was okay. I managed to give them a few comments that, if not useful, at least showed some degree of insight into the work, some sense that I understood more or less what they were trying to do. And they liked my poem, so that gave me a bit of confidence.

After I'd met with this group a few times, I began to feel more comfortable. These people were all trying to produce poems with a high level of craft, just like I was. We could all read the poems in *The Best American Poetry* and

Try to see yourself from the outside, and evaluate yourself the way other people do: by what you've done. That will tell you who your peers are. Give yourself permission to belong with them.

understand them, more or less, eventually, and appreciate them. We all taught workshops or did events in the literary community. I wasn't so different from them after all, although I still felt they were somehow above me.

But one night, I learned that everyone else also had trouble finishing the homework in time for class, and I realized that these people were my peers. After that, I forced myself to sit up straight and remember that I belonged. I didn't feel it, but I made myself act like it and remember it was true. That changed my experience of the group immediately for the better. And over time, as I kept acting like I belonged and reminding myself that objectively I did belong, I began to actually feel like I belonged.

It's still challenging to be part of this group, but it's also a relief to find peers. What I want to highlight is that I had to claim them as my peers. It would have been possible, even easy, to sit at that table and say, "I don't belong here; these people are at a higher level than I am" because I didn't *feel* as competent and accomplished as they *looked*. But I have worked very hard for a lot of years to see myself from the outside, to try to make judgements based not on how I feel but on objective, observable facts.* Based on data from the physical world, these people are

---

* See "Keep a Compliments List" on page 58.

my peers. The growth moment for me is to accept that, to claim my place at the table.

It's important to look for people you can claim as your peers, because it helps you understand who you are and what you can do.

Who are you equal to, even if you don't feel like you are?

Try to see yourself from the outside, and evaluate yourself the way other people do: by what you've done.* That will tell you who your peers are. Give yourself permission to belong with them.

---

* See "You're Probably More Qualified Than You Feel" on page 94.

KEEP A COMPLIMENTS LIST

If you want to increase your confidence, then "claim your peers" sounds like a great idea.* "See yourself from the outside" seems like useful advice. But how do you do it? How do you escape from the ever-so-true-seeming way that you *feel* about yourself? It's easy to say "see yourself objectively and make decisions based on that," but, to paraphrase one of Anthony Francis's characters, "Nice strategy. Got any tactics?"**

Here is a tactic. It has changed my life. Try it and see if it changes yours, too. My mentor Samantha Bennett recommends this in her very useful book *Get It Done*. Give it a year to really work its magic. Here's what you do: keep a list of the compliments people give you.

---

* See "Claim Your Peers" on page 54.

** *"Oh, now that, that's smart strategy, ma'am,"* Gould muttered. *"Got any tactics?"* From a story by Anthony Francis, set in the steampunk universe that includes the novel *Jeremiah Willstone and the Clockwork Time Machine*.

People are saying amazing stuff about you. All the time.

Pick a Place

If you want to try this, decide right now where you're going to write down the first one. You can always change it later. Even if you only write them down willy-nilly on napkins and receipts, and then lose them, this could still make a difference for you, so don't let the place put you off from doing it. I write my compliments in a document in my writing software*, but you could try a note on your phone or a special notebook. I don't recommend a page in your journal, because you're going to use up your journal and get a new one. Just decide what you'll start with, and start. You can refine as you go.

Do This

Every time someone compliments you, write down the actual words they said as a generalized description of yourself. For example, your friend says, "You're so creative." You write on the list:

Creative

Your sister says, "You look great today." You write:

Looks great

---

* For my latest recommendations of writing software, and other resources, see see *www.KeikoOLeary.com/writing-resources/*

If someone compliments a group you are in, this also counts. For example, a workshop teacher says, "Thanks, everyone, for being so attentive." You write:

Attentive

When the compliment isn't easily rendered as an adjective or verb phrase, you can use a sentence. (My examples use feminine pronouns, but of course you'd use your own pronouns.) For example, someone says "I love the backs of your postcards." You write:

People love the backs of her postcards.

Even things that don't feel like compliments can go on the list. Someone writes you back to say they're sorry they can't attend your workshop. You write:

People are sorry when they can't attend her workshops.

Sure, you can think they're just being polite. But really? People are busy. If they took the time out of their day to write that they're sorry they can't attend your workshop, I'm pretty sure you can truthfully add that compliment to your list.

If someone says something in a way you can't stand to alter, just add it as a quote. For example, you can put something like this into your list:

"Just staying in touch with you and the prompts and the group keeps me happy."

You don't have to change it to "Just staying in touch with her and the prompts and the group keeps people happy."

It's sometimes a fun writing exercise to figure out how to make something match the format of the list.

You can also add things that aren't something someone said, but something they did. For example, a writing friend mentions a story you wrote years ago. You write:

People remember her stories.

You could keep a separate compliments list about your work, but it's probably best to start off with a general list to make it easier and therefore more likely that you'll use the list.

What Will Happen Right Away

First, you'll start actually noticing what people say about you. Sometimes when people give us compliments, our experience is *this person said something nice about me*. If your reaction is embarrassment, the compliments list can help you feel less embarrassed over time. But even if you feel good, it might be a very general feeling. You don't take in the specifics. This is keeping you from knowing how other people experience you. Compliments are data about your external identity. You are wasting that information if all you do with them is feel good or embarrassed. It's so different to think, *Oh, they said something nice*, versus *Wow, someone's impression of me is that I "hold faithfully over the years."*

What Will Happen Over Time

Even if you never reread your list, just writing down these snippets of other people's experience of you will slowly reveal trends in what people see in you, and allow you to claim them.

But maybe sometime you will reread your compliments list. I did that a while back, when it was at 2,822 words. After the first couple of screens, I sort of started to numb out and think, "Who is this amazing person I'm reading about?" Then I thought, "Oh right, this is me."

People are saying amazing stuff about you, too! All the time. Only you don't notice. If you suffer from low self-esteem or impostor syndrome, keeping a compliments list will help because it allows you to see yourself from the outside. And if you feel just fine about yourself, the list will still help you understand how people see you.

You can start right now with this compliment: your writing matters.

We are all just trying to do something that matters, and we can't do it most of the time. But still, sometimes we can, and that's the part that all the other times are for.

THE REAL LIFE OF FICTION

Whenever I ask the question "How shall I live?" I always look to literature for the answer. But this time the answer came in a dream.

The dream took place in an auditorium, an old one, like the Century movie theaters in San José: a huge domed room, with plush maroon carpet that matched the seats.* Some of the seats held members of my writing group. We were there because our fellow member Anthony was going to read an excerpt from his novel, and I was supposed to introduce him.

I was standing on a wooden stage, behind a podium. This was a writing conference, titled The Real Life of Fiction.

---

* I always love it when I can go visit a place I read about in a book. The Century theaters are closed now, but at least one of the domes was still standing when this book went to print. They are right next to the Winchester Mystery House. And if you want to read a novel that has both those places in it, you could try *Vanishing Point* by Michaela Roessner.

I had notes, but they didn't help. I babbled. I forgot the title of the novel. I forgot the name of the conference. At one point, through the haze of my stammering incompetence, I saw clearly for a moment: in the front row, a woman with the curly hair and Coke-bottle glasses that could only belong to one of my favorite authors: *Oh no*, I thought, *not only am I messing up, but Connie Willis is seeing it*.

I was holding a copy of Anthony's book, a yellow-edged pocket paperback, the old kind that maybe a Frederik Pohl novel would be inside of. The cover, too, matched that golden-age-of-science-fiction style: white block lettering arcing over an orange and ochre sunset that led up to a sky full of stars. It wasn't one of the novels Anthony has actually published, but in the dream I'd read it.

The microphone was from the 1930s. Its metallic workings distorted my voice. The audience stared at me. Connie Willis's glasses stared at me. I kept talking, even though I had forgotten the name of the conference and the title of the novel. Then I remembered to say that Anthony writes like the cinema.

I tried to explain what that meant, and my words made no sense. But I realized that since Anthony was about to read from his novel, I didn't have to explain. I said, "You'll see in a minute anyway. I don't have to tell you." I stepped down as Anthony stood up. I walked toward the seats as he made his way to the podium, a twin copy of the novel in his hand. He smiled and thanked me as we passed.

I'd done a terrible job, but I was happy, because it was the best I could do.

I'd babbled and stammered, but I'd said what mattered: that the conference was important, and that Anthony writes like the cinema. And that we work together in our writing group. After I sat down, I remembered I was supposed to have said more about the writing group, that someone had told me I should use this opportunity to advertise it. *Oh well*, I thought, *next time*.

What is "the real life of fiction"? Here is my answer: I am not content to read fiction or even to write it. I will not be satisfied unless I live it. I want my life to be a story, which means I have to transcend myself and do what matters in the critical moment.

But there is no shortcut, and sometimes you can't do what maybe you should do, or what you see other people can do. At my writing group, I see Betsy just do things she thinks might work, like run a crowdfunding campaign; I see David just write novel after novel as though he has every right to do it. I even see myself posting videos that I hope no one will watch, but that a year ago I wouldn't have even dared to record. Sometimes your skills aren't where you wish they were, sometimes you don't know the story you're living, but that is not an excuse to avoid action.

You have to do what you can, because that is the only way ever to be able to do something that matters. The videos I make next year will be better, but only if I make these videos now.

There is a connection here to literature, to mythology, to Orpheus and Odysseus and Leopold Bloom,* because we are all just trying to do something that matters, and we can't do it most of the time. But still, sometimes we can, and that's the part that all the other times are for. That's the part that makes our life a story.

What is the real life of fiction? It's the real life of the times when we can. It's the times when we can't, all condensed into a single scene; it's the maroon carpet seats in the dome theater and the echo of an old microphone. It's everything you do so that you can do the one thing that matters; it's the one thing shining and then passing away.

Do what you can, and do it now. The real life of fiction is the real life of real life.

---

* The protagonist of James Joyce's *Ulysses*.

THE PARABLE OF DON MCLEAN
OR
WHY ENCOURAGE EVERYONE, INCLUDING YOURSELF

There's some quote about a famous writer; they asked her whether she thought creative writing programs (or something) discouraged young writers, and her response was "not enough of them." I interpret this to mean that if more writers were discouraged early on and quit writing, then we wouldn't have so many so-called bad writers. This may be clever, but it is misguided.

Here's why I disagree, and why I encourage everyone: you never know who is Don McLean.

You've heard of Don McLean, right? The guy who wrote the masterpiece "American Pie," a song that has transcended the events it is based on, that has touched the lives of people across generations? He also made a pretty great song about van Gogh's painting *The Starry Night*. But here's the thing: every other song he ever made was bad. Horrible. Okay, I don't know, maybe you like Don

McLean. Maybe I'd like him if I gave him another chance. All I know is that one time I thought *if he can write "American Pie" and "Vincent," his other songs must be good*. So I found a Best Of album and listened to it, only to be sorely disappointed. All the lyrics are cheesy. And these are the Best Of! So that means there are many more songs he wrote that are worse! But the point is, I am glad he wrote all those bad songs because maybe some of them helped him become the person who could write "American Pie." I welcome all those other songs into the world because they give me "American Pie."

You can't use the "not enough of them" logic when somebody could be Don McLean. You've got to encourage everyone, no matter how terrible you think their work is, because you never know what they might create someday. And if even one of their pieces is someone's "American Pie," all that bad work will have been worth it.

They don't even have to write something that becomes well known. I think a piece of art is worth making even if it only ever touches one person in the whole universe. Because that person needs it.

Also, our world is so interconnected, so mysterious, so full of unexpected results, that you can't know the full effect of any person's work. Maybe some obscure poem that never touched anyone else gave Don McLean something he needed, without which he never could have written "American Pie." And maybe that poem would never

Encourage everyone, no matter how terrible you think their work is, because you never know what they might create someday.

have existed if the poet hadn't experienced some other obscure piece. There's a lovely picture book, *Because* by Mo Willems, that shows how the spirit of art gets passed from one artist to another, causing new art to be created in every genre.

What if someone had discouraged Don McLean, or the person who wrote the hypothetical obscure poem? We wouldn't have "American Pie." I'm not okay with that. So please encourage everyone, including yourself. We all hope to create many pieces that become well known, that touch many people, that make a difference in the world. But that is not guaranteed. What is guaranteed is that if you let yourself write, you have a chance.

GET RESULTS FASTER BY USING BRIGHT SPOTS

Once upon a time, I thought I was bad at finishing. After all, I had only published four articles on the Write to the End blog in three years.* I really wanted to publish regularly, but I didn't know how to make myself do it. Using the "bright spot" method described here, I created a system that got me publishing a blog post nearly every month for the next three years. Here's how I did it, and how you can apply the method to achieve your own results.

The idea is to look for "bright spots"—places where you're already succeeding—and then to apply what you learn to solving the problem at hand. It's more likely to get results because it's based on what's already working *for you*.**

---

* Write to the End is my writing group. See "We Welcome All Writing" on page 14 for an introduction to it.

** This idea comes from the book *Switch: How to Change Things When Change Is Hard* by Chip Heath and Dan Heath. All the

I started to look for places where I actually did finish things so that I could try to duplicate any success that I found. I didn't expect to find much. I was wrong.

Bright Spot 1: Serving Dinner

The first bright spot I discovered was dinner. I produced and served dinner, every day, pretty much at 6 p.m. Here was an example of successful and consistent daily finishing! So I wasn't bad at finishing after all. I continued to analyze the bright spot: why did I succeed at "getting dinner published" every night at 6 p.m., but not at finishing creative projects?

Because people in my house needed to eat, and they couldn't eat much later than 6 p.m. Aha! I'd discovered two project characteristics that help me finish:

- An external deadline.
- An audience—other people counting on me to deliver.

How could I use this discovery to help myself finish more creative projects? In particular, how could I help myself publish more articles? I didn't know, so I went back to looking for bright spots.

---

books I've read by these authors are fun to read and full of useful practices.

Bright Spot 2: Sending a Newsletter

The next bright spot I discovered was even more valuable because it related to writing. I'd been sending the Write to the End newsletter (in one form or another) for over 10 years. Here was another example of successful and consistent finishing, and it was actually an example of successful and consistent publishing. The newsletter had the same two helpful characteristics as serving dinner: an external deadline and an audience. I had discovered the Serving Dinner Model of Publishing, and I was already using it successfully!*

Finding the Solution

I suddenly knew how I could help myself publish consistently on the writing group's blog. It was terrifying to commit to this, but I did it. I added a section for new blog posts to the newsletter, and I decided there would always be at least one new article in that section.

It worked! After I made that plan, I succeeded at writing and publishing a new article every month, because I had linked that behavior to the two helpful characteristics my bright spots had revealed: a deadline and an audience. And I lived happily ever after (at least until the next problem).

---

* Feel free to try out this model, detailed in "The Serving Dinner Model of Publishing" on page 84.

Your Own Bright Spots

Bright spots can help you achieve a result you want by using solutions that are already working in other areas.

What's a result you want to achieve? Use bright spots to decide what to try next. Pay attention to your own life and notice where you are already succeeding at something similar. What characteristics or environmental factors accompany that success? Try to think of an approach that incorporates what you learned from those bright spots.

I wish you success in your own bright spot story.

DON'T SHOW YOUR WORK TO YOUR FRIENDS

What's the right thing to say to someone who has just shown you a manuscript of the worst prose you've ever seen, which they say is a story, but you can hardly even find a character, let alone discern a plot?

Wait, I'll make it worse: they're looking at you expectantly, as innocent as a baby seal waiting to be clubbed.

Hold on a sec, it's still not bad enough: you like this person very much and have known them for years. Maybe you even love them. Maybe you live in the same house.

Okay, now go ahead: what's the right thing to say?

৯

This is why you shouldn't show your work to your friends.

Perhaps you've already made this mistake, and people have said mean things about your work. Remember, they didn't know what to do! They were doing their best to help. Let's try to forgive them.

∽

Everybody has to start where they are. If you want to make masterful work, you have to start by making unskilled work. If you don't believe me, and you like Harlan Ellison's fiction, go find a copy of his collected stories and read the one about the snake.* "But he was a kid when he wrote that," you say. Yeah, and he was also a beginning writer.

What would you say to the young Harlan Ellison, if he showed you that story? I bet you have no trouble coming up with an answer this time, because you're thinking of a kid (even if it's Harlan Ellison). I bet you would say something like, "Wow, you wrote a story! How about you write another one?" And I bet you would mean it.

And you know what else? I bet it would be exactly the right thing to say.

---

* "The Gloconda" in *The Essential Ellison* (either edition works).

Everybody has to start where they are. If you want to make masterful work, you have to start by making unskilled work.

YOU CAN NEVER SAY THANK YOU

The first book I ever bought about how to be a writer was Anne Lamott's *Bird by Bird*. I was lucky, because that book is perfect for me. I am rereading it yet again, and it's as though she's right there, speaking only to me, telling me exactly what I need to know right now, just like all the other times I've read it.

If somebody writes a book like that, or creates anything that touches you, it's natural to get the urge to say thank you. And what that looks like for me is writing hundreds of unfinished letters inside my head, and rehearsing what I'd say if I ever met the author, revising it over and over, to try to convey how much her book has meant to me. And believing that if I could just say thank you that I would feel relief from this terrible debt of gratitude and be able to accept the gift of her book and go on with my life.

But here's the thing: I met Anne Lamott last spring, and I got to talk to her twice: once just passing by in the bookstore where she was teaching, and once after I'd waited in line for 45 minutes to get her book signed. And both times, I tried to say thank you. I *did* say, "Thank you." I said, "Your book changed my life." I said, "I got your book when it first came out." I said, "I've reread it many times, and it always makes a difference for me." I said the right things the first time, but I still felt the need to say thank you. I said them again the second time, but I still felt the need to say thank you. She was gracious and kind both times, but Anne Lamott is wise, and I got the feeling that maybe she knew I was attempting something futile.

I know I did the right thing to try, but I left feeling worse than ever, because there was no way I could convey, even to the author, my experience of her book and how much it has meant to me. There was no way I could make her experience what I experience when I read her book, no way to make her feel the love she transmitted to me through her words. She wrote it; she is herself. She can't read it as me. She can't feel what I felt and experience how she changed me. I hope you understand what I mean, because I can't say it any more ways.

If you're feeling the urge to say thank you, you're in a difficult situation. In order to repay your debt of gratitude, you need the person to experience what you experienced. That is impossible, so you are out of luck.

Except.

Except that they *did* experience what you experienced. They read something else, by someone else, and they experienced it. Or they saw a painting or heard a piece of music or read a mathematical proof, and they were touched and felt the same debt of gratitude that you feel. And then later they created the thing that passed that experience on to you. And therefore, the only way that you can ever repay this debt is by creating something that passes it on to the next person. And then maybe they will try to say thank you and fail. And you can never know if what you made succeeded, because even when people say thank you, they can never convey their experience, and you will never experience it back from your own work.

There is no guarantee. But you owe the debt already, so you must try. Write what's in you to write; create what's in you to create; and release your work. Create, and have faith that what you create could touch someone. It's the only way you can ever say thank you.

Have faith that what you create could touch someone.

THE SERVING DINNER MODEL OF PUBLISHING

Do you have a pile of unfinished pieces? Would you like to find a way to finish more projects? Important: it's normal for creative people to start many more projects than they finish, so please never feel bad about that pile again. But you can improve your rate of finishing.

Finish More Projects

Using "bright spots,"* I discovered that a project with two simple characteristics is much easier to finish:

1. An external deadline.

2. An audience—other people counting on you to deliver.

Students in my classes have found this model effective for a wide variety of projects, but I named it "the Serving Dinner Model of Publishing" because of how I discovered it. Every day, about 6 p.m. (a deadline), my family (an

---

* See "Get Results Faster by Using Bright Spots" on page 73.

audience) needs to eat dinner. Therefore, I succeed at "publishing" dinner every day around 6 p.m.

Here are some examples of how you can apply the Serving Dinner Model in order to finish something.

One-Time Projects

As part of Thinking Ink Press, I create Instant Books (mini books folded from a single sheet of paper).* My first two ideas for Instant Books are still unfinished, but in the meantime I produced three others, plus three or four postcards, each with a complete short story. Why did I not finish the first two projects, but I did finish the others? It's because I applied the Serving Dinner Model to the ones I finished. I caused the two helpful conditions to exist by saying to my partners, "I'll make *Jagged Fragments* for Anthony to sell at the Clockwork Alchemy convention," and "I'll make *Bees* for Betsy to sell at Play on Words." Boom! Instant deadline and audience.

My first two Instant Book ideas have never had an upcoming author event associated with them, so I have had trouble setting aside other things to work on them. But I want to finish them, so I will be looking for opportunities to apply the Serving Dinner Model.

---

* You can see them at
www.thinkinginkpress.com/instant-books/

A project with two simple characteristics is much easier to finish:
1. An external deadline.
2. An audience—other people counting on you to deliver.

EXAMPLES OF ONE-TIME PROJECTS:

- Produce a small edition of a short piece to sell at a particular event.
- Schedule your self-published book to come out on a certain date, and allow presales. (Only recommended if you have self-published before and have enough experience to meet your deadline.)
- Commit to reading at an open mic. Finish your piece so that you can read it there.
- Participate in an organized challenge such as National Novel Writing Month.

I realize that some of these sound stressful. They are. It's the healthy kind of stress that helps you be productive.

Recurring Projects

The Serving Dinner Model can also be applied to recurring projects.

I applied this model to my writing group's blog by promising to deliver a new article every time I sent the group's newsletter. If you can get people counting on you to produce something every week or every month, this can be very helpful for finishing recurring projects such as blog posts. If you can get someone to hire you, that's even better! This could be in a more traditional context, such as getting hired to write a column, or a more entrepreneurial context, such as using an online service where supporters pledge a certain amount of money each month, and you deliver an agreed-upon product on a schedule (for example, one short story per week).

EXAMPLES OF RECURRING PROJECTS:

- Newsletters or other subscriptions.
- Columns and other recurring products.
- Multisession classes. You will be forced to produce the content for each class meeting. Perhaps this content is a handout or a chapter of your how-to book.
- Sections or chapters. One way to get an audience for these is to find a writing partner. If you agree to deliver a new chapter each Friday, that gives you an audience and a deadline.

Try It

Would you like to try the Serving Dinner Model?

It's probably best to pick something small for the first time. What's one thing you've been wanting to produce?

For that particular project, how can you get an external deadline and an audience counting on you?

Set your deadline. Make an agreement with your audience.

Start cooking.

THE GREEKS DON'T OWN THE STARS

I met my friend Jessica when we were both on Education Abroad in Chile. Her astrological sign is Scorpio, and she'd always wanted to see the constellation but never had.

One time we took a trip to Valparaíso, and we ended up sitting on the beach at night with a bunch of people we'd just met, drinking cheap wine from a box. There was this guy who liked Jessica, but he was a little too drunk for her to like him back. He said, "*me encantas*" (literally, you enchant me), and she was sort of flattered and sort of horrified. He asked her what her sign was, and she told him.

"Ah, Scorpio," he said. He pointed up at a little Y of stars. "That's Scorpio." He tried to put his arms around her, but she refused. She was enchanted, but not by him. She gazed up at the stars, finally seeing her own constellation for the first time.

As we walked home that night, Jessica was still looking at the stars. "This feels so magical," she said.

"I'm connected to the Southern Hemisphere now." I felt connected, too.

Later we found out that the constellation was not Scorpio after all. Two of the stars in the Y are actually Alpha and Beta Centauri. In a way, that connects us even more, because those stars can only be seen in the Southern Hemisphere. Jessica was disappointed that she still had not seen Scorpio (which turns out not even to be named Scorpio but rather Scorpius), but eventually we did some research, and we discovered that Scorpius is easily visible on summer nights in California, so now we see it every year. And since I also travel to Chile to visit my husband's family, I get to see Alpha and Beta Centauri, and the private constellation I still call Jessica's Scorpio.

༺

The sky is full of stories. And not just the traditional stories, Orion and Scorpius, Andromeda and Perseus. The sky is full of private stories, overlapping stories, your stories. The traditional constellations are not the only constellations: the Greeks don't own the stars. The astronomers don't own the stars, either. The stars belong to all of us.

༺

I have another private constellation, which I call the Brontosaurus. I only saw it for sure one time, on a highway

Your personal geography
is a wellspring of memoir
and poetry, and a source of
authentic detail for fiction.

in the Nevada desert, looking out the back window of my mom's 1969 Chevy Malibu. I was 10 years old, the year before I got glasses and learned that normal people can see individual leaves on trees from a moving car. I've looked for the Brontosaurus many times since then, and my best hypothesis is that it shares stars with Canis Major, but I've never been sure.

I used this private constellation in a short story, as an orienting constellation for a time traveler. I put it in during the first draft, thinking I'd find something better later, but it ended up fitting the story, because the two characters turn out to be the same person, just as the *Brontosaurus* fossil turned out to be a fossil of an already-identified animal that had already been named *Apatosaurus*.*

Maybe you've never had a private constellation, but you still have a source of stories that's as deep and wide as the sky. Any place you've known has stories embedded in its geography. Think of the geography of the place you grew up, I mean the very local geography. I grew up in an apartment fourplex that shared a driveway with another fourplex. The bottlebrush tree in front of our window held many stories: the time I climbed it and discovered I was allergic to bottlebrush; the time a cricket sat in it and kept

---

* Recent research suggests that *Brontosaurus* and *Apatosaurus* might be different after all. Wow!

us awake all night with its singing; the time my sister and I used it to make a blanket fort in which we ate an entire box of Donkey Kong cereal.

Your personal geography is a wellspring of memoir and poetry, and a source of authentic detail for fiction. It's a place you can go to find solace or horror, pain or relief. There's nothing like real life for sheer bandwidth, the amount of information that can be delivered and stored.

Think of a small place you know, or an object you've used many times: the front window of your childhood home, a tree, a silverware drawer, a hill. You can unpack stories from this place, this object. And those stories will be filled with authentic details, sense impressions, feelings specific to a place and time. In short, what literature is made of.

ൠ

When you need stories, when you need details, when you need emotions, look to the physical world, or the physical world in your memory. I promise you'll find something there, maybe even the perfect constellation.

YOU'RE PROBABLY MORE QUALIFIED THAN YOU FEEL

Do you sometimes feel like you're not qualified for something that other people think you're qualified for? I've found a way to test.

Recently I presented at a Prolific Writers Life conference, as part of a panel titled "Traditional Publishing: Big or Small, It's All Business."

When I met the other people on the panel, my first thought was *Help! They are out of my league.*

I already knew Judy Gitenstein is a big New York editor, but the other panelists are also impressive: Julie Fast has sold over 500,000 copies of her books, Jennifer Wilkov is a sought-after speaker, and our moderator Tanya Brockett has a thriving book coaching and editing business. I have a small press with a few books and tiny revenue, and I don't even spend much time on the business side. My mind started looking for a way to get out of the conference.

Then I remembered I struggle with impostor syndrome.

The best defense against impostor syndrome is this: you don't have to act on your feelings. You can instead act according to the evidence.

There's a TED Talk by Valerie Young, in which she says that people with impostor syndrome feel like they have to be great at everything in order to deserve their position, but in reality it's okay to be bad at some things.* She also says feelings are the last thing to change, and you have to act your way into that change.

It's hard to tell the difference between impostor syndrome and not being qualified. They both *feel* the same. But I remembered to look at the evidence. Based on the physical evidence, did I have something to offer the audience of this panel?

I decided to write down true and neutral statements about my qualifications, and then evaluate those statements the way an outside observer would. For example, one feeling I had was *my press is so tiny no one would care about it*, but a true and neutral statement is *I run a small press*. To an outside observer, someone who runs a small press belongs on a panel about traditional publishing. In fact, "Small" was even in the title of the panel.

Another feeling I had was *I don't see very many submissions, and who knows if my taste is good*, but a true and neutral statement is *I am an acquisitions editor*. I have experience receiving submissions and evaluating them. Many writers could benefit from understanding more about what I do.

---

* "Thinking your way out of imposter syndrome" from TEDNYC Idea Search 2017, *www.youtube.com/watch?v=h7v-GG3SEWQ*

Through writing down true and neutral statements, I became willing to stay on the panel. I forced myself to take the perspective that I didn't have to know everything, that it was okay to just know what I knew. I saw that I could still contribute value with the experience I had.

It's important to note that I was still worried. I still didn't *feel* like I belonged on the panel, but I did it anyway, because the *evidence* said I belonged. And, when I was actually doing the panel, I had a great time, and my contribution helped people in the audience.

The best defense against impostor syndrome is this: you don't have to act on your feelings. You can instead act according to the evidence.

If you struggle with feeling unqualified, try this process of writing down true and neutral statements. You might need to do it with a friend who can help you check if you're being true and neutral. They can also help you take the perspective of an outside observer.

But what if you write down true and neutral statements, and it turns out you're unqualified? First, I'd recommend getting confirmation from someone you can trust to be objective, because it's possible that you're not actually making true and neutral statements, or that your feelings are affecting your ability to evaluate the evidence.

However, if you and your objective helper decide that you really are not qualified, you have to look at the specific situation and try to find a solution. I know that in applying for jobs, you definitely should apply anyway even if you don't have everything they ask for. And in general, if you know you tend to underestimate yourself, you should probably err on the side of going for it anyway. I don't know what your specific situation is, but let's at least look at an example.

Let's say my panel was "Big Publishing: How to Get a Book Deal." I am not qualified to be on that panel, because I don't have any direct experience with big publishing book deals. What are my options? I could do the panel anyway and either stay mostly silent or pretend I knew what I was talking about and say random stuff that could mislead the audience—but I'm not okay with either of those options. Being dishonest or not giving value is exactly what the feeling of being unqualified is trying to prevent.

What are ethical options? I could contact the conference organizers and ask them to change the focus of the panel so that I fit: for example, "Big or Small Publishing: How to Get a Book Deal." I could ask them to put me on a different panel. Or I could resign from the panel and do something else for the conference. I couldn't become an expert in big publishing quickly enough for this conference, but in some other situations, improving your skills could be an option.

I'm sure you can find a solution that will match your situation. But I'm also pretty sure that you're usually in the other situation, the one where you are qualified but don't *feel* qualified. When that happens, I hope you'll remember to test your qualifications by writing down true and neutral statements. Now I'm going to give you a compliment.* Go ahead and take it in, and add it to your compliments list: you're more qualified than you feel.

---

* See "Keep a Compliments List" on page 58.

I promise to write, but I also promise to live, and I ask you to do the same.

NO *ENTERPRISE*

Warning: This essay contains a very minor spoiler (not plot significant) for the third book in the Bloody Jack Adventures series by L.A. Meyer.

I'm in the movie theater watching *Star Trek: Beyond*. I haven't turned off my expectations, and I'm finding much to complain about. But although my mind is churning on dialogue problems and weird plot choices, my main experience is this: my heart wants to come out of my chest and go to the screen. I don't know these new characters; I keep comparing them to the originals; I don't understand them at all. But they are on the *Enterprise*, and I feel a gravitational pull to be there too.

Later I'm crying, and it's not because of the events of the movie. It's not even because Leonard Nimoy is dead. I've known that fact for over a year, and my mind can finally almost touch it, but not quite, certainly not enough to cry. No, this is something more fundamental: I'm crying because *Star Trek* isn't real. I can't live there. There is no *Enterprise*.

Where can I find consolation? Where can I learn what I should do in the face of this problem? Of course I look to literature for the answer. Here's what I find: In *Under the Jolly Roger*, L.A. Meyer puts Jacky Faber on the *Pequod*, even though his novel is historical fiction and the *Pequod* is a fictional ship. Why does he do that? It's so he can live in *Moby Dick*, through his character. By putting her on the *Pequod*, he refuses to be left out of fiction; he declares that we're all the same, and that we're all in the same world, whether we be fictional or whatever the other thing is.

So, Mr. Meyer, I thank you for this comforting hypothesis. And I see that, in a way, I live in *Star Trek* when I experience *Star Trek* stories. I see that if I were an officer on the *Enterprise*, I wouldn't be living in *Star Trek* the story, I'd be living a life on the *Enterprise*. But still, in the theater the feeling is visceral: my whole body is straining toward the screen—I belong there, not here.

Writing this, I realize: the feeling isn't that I belong in space, or even on the *Enterprise*. It's that I belong in a story. It comes down to that. I've never seen it so clearly before.

What makes *your* heart swell? What makes your soul want to come out of your body and go *there*, more than anywhere else? I love Rembrandt, I love van Gogh, and my heart moves toward *The Starry Night*. But it moves toward *Star Trek* more, toward stories more. I love linguistics and math, and my heart moves toward them, but they are mainly loves of the mind. I love making books and origami, but that is mainly a love of the body, of fingers and eyes. The place that pulls my soul out of my chest is fiction, is words, is story. Literature is my first and truest love. I can't deny that anymore. I must make it my first priority. What must you make yours?

There's a fashion for saying to do only your top thing and ignore everything else. But if you need to be creative, doing only your top thing doesn't work. You have to live in order to get ideas. You have to go deep in other areas if you want to make breakthroughs in your area of specialty.

If you love writing, but it's not your top thing, keep writing. Maybe write a little less and do your top thing a little more, but keep writing. Keep coming to Write to the End or going to your own writing group. What you do there will help you do your top thing.

I won't stop making nonwritten art, doing other things I love, living in the moments I'm not writing. What a gift this world is; what varied and wonderful opportunities it contains: not only to read and to write, not only to study the things I love, but also the meaningfulness of pure experience—to touch the texture of a 20-year-old construction paper cover I made for *Uhura's Song*,[*] to hear slow crickets at 2 a.m., to feel the lemony squeeze of

---

[*] A *Star Trek: The Original Series* novel by Janet Kagan.

tears beginning to form, to look into the night sky and find Antares and recognize the constellation that's not Jessica's Scorpio, but to think of it, and her, and the times we spent together.[*] Life, if I let myself open to it, is like being in a story.

I promise to write, but I also promise to live, and I ask you to do the same. Do your top thing, and put it first, but let the rest of your life flower, too. The other things you love, the care and depth with which you do them, the appreciation you give to the passing and irretrievable moments of this one life—all will return to you and help you as you work on your top thing, and your life will become a story.

Promise me you'll do it.

There is no *Enterprise* but the one we make ourselves.

---

[*] See "The Greeks Don't Own the Stars" on page 89.

HOW TO BELIEVE IN YOURSELF

I got a fortune cookie last time that said, "Believe in yourself and others will too." That's probably true, but it's not very helpful as advice. Because if you don't believe in yourself, how can you start? People who already believe in themselves will say, "Just do it. Just believe in yourself." But this is the same as saying, "I don't know."

Here's how to believe in yourself, which is backward from the fortune cookie: hang around with people who believe in you, and eventually you will believe in yourself. This is the reason you need a writing group.

And not just any writing group. You need a group like Write to the End: one that's full of people who believe in you. This is possible within many different writing group structures, but I think it's easier to find in a structure like ours, one that's focused on writing rather than on critique.

In our group, we write together, share what we write, and encourage each other to keep going. Every Tuesday, people I admire and respect act like it's normal to write, and act like it matters that I write, and act like what I write matters. That process alone helps people come to believe in themselves, or to believe in themselves more.

But because we meet every week, there are other moments, too. When my arms were injured, Betsy typed up the first draft of one of my stories. Sometimes I still boggle over that: why? Why would anyone possibly do that? (Though I'd do it for any of us, and I bet you would, too.) Also, she sent me an email to say she's glad I'm planning to publish flash fiction. The logic is inescapable: she believes in me. Other group members do other actions that have the same inescapable conclusion: they believe in me. And it's working: it is forcing me to believe in myself.

What If You Don't Have a Writing Group?

If you want a writing group, you can find one or start one. It's not that hard, though it could take some time before everything's running smoothly.

But you don't have to wait to start the process of believing in yourself. Every time you write, you're giving your brain a data point that implies you believe in yourself. And reading books like this one also helps: I am a real person speaking to you in text, and your brain knows that. Read encouraging books, write often, and start the process of finding a writing group.

I believe in you. You will come to believe in yourself. Keep going.

Hang around with people who believe in you, and eventually you will believe in yourself.

WRITING PEOPLE OFF

I don't write people off. If you talk to me, I will encourage you to write. (Or I'll encourage you to make art, or create smartphone apps, or start a business, or make whatever it is you want to make. But usually the people I meet want to write.) But if I were the kind of person who writes people off, this would be my top five list.

1. You want to know your first short story will sell before you deign to write a first draft.

2. You are in love with your idea for a novel, and your idea of yourself as the author of it, but you aren't working on it in any way.

3. You send me email after email about how you are going to come to the writing group, but you just want this or that special reassurance, or to meet with me privately (again), or to explain some particular of your situation that you think matters—but none of it matters. What matters is that you write. I care nothing for your problems or your diagnoses. Write. Come to

the group if you want, or find another group. Write. Quit sending me email unless it's a manuscript.

4. You corner me and won't stop talking about this book you think I should write using your material. Go write it yourself, I say. I don't know what you want, but I actually think it is not for a book to exist about your ideas. I think you just want to watch someone act like they agree with you. I'll bet if you start writing, this will go away.

5. I'm sure I belong on this list. I'm like #3 whenever I don't write but instead look for reassurances. I'm like #4 whenever I talk someone's ear off about my ideas but don't work on them. I'm like #2 whenever I don't write but fantasize instead. I'm like #1 whenever I want to know I'll end up with a story before I'm willing to put pen to paper. And here's another thing I do, which can be #5: I have all these ambitions and even talent, I write stuff that I want to publish, but I just let it sit around in a notebook or on a hard drive.

Luckily I never write anyone off, not even myself. I keep going no matter what, because attendance is my superpower. I am mean to myself; I tell myself I'll never succeed; I yell at myself for how bad my writing is and how abysmally I manage my time and skill. But being mean to oneself could be #6 on this list! I'm sure it has never helped anyone to write. I am going to stop being mean and treat myself the way I treat everyone else.

I will always encourage you if you want to write. I promise to encourage myself, too.

COLORLESS GREEN IDEAS CRASHED MY CAR
OR
YOUR RIGHT TO SAY THINGS THAT DON'T MAKE SENSE

The structure of language gives us the power to say things that don't make sense: ideas can't have color (or crash a car), and something colorless can't also be green, but I can say "colorless green ideas crashed my car," and you can understand me, even if you're not quite sure what I mean.* The syntax of the sentence makes sense, so you're going to start forming hypotheses about how the sentence can be true: maybe the "ideas" are aliens, and they are transparent but also green. By using syntax that people are used to, you can write about something that no one has ever experienced, and people will experience it through your writing.

---

* "Colorless green ideas" is a phrase from a famous example in Noam Chomsky's book *Syntactic Structures*.

Meaning is not dependent on making sense.

If I break the syntax—"green a the car colorless my"—you might not be able to follow what I'm saying anymore. This string of words doesn't follow the rules of English, so it makes even less sense than "colorless green ideas."

However, with enough structure of other sorts, unorthodox syntax can create deep meaning. For example, e.e. cummings:

> anyone lived in a pretty how town
> (with up so floating many bells down). *

Meaning is not dependent on making sense. Meaning exists even in things that don't "make sense." The e.e. cummings poem I quoted above doesn't "make sense" (the syntax is weird, the words are used in ways you've never seen before), but its meaning is there nonetheless. In fact, we could argue that its true meaning and effect are only possible *because* cummings breaks the syntax and does things in this unconventional way. I'm sure it took him a long time and many revisions to get that poem into its final state.

When you're editing a piece and the effect you want to create requires breaking syntax or creating an unconventional story structure, or doing something else that doesn't "make sense," do it! Your loyalty is not to

---

* Excerpt from "anyone lived in a pretty how town" by e.e. cummings.

some social or literary convention, but to the entity you are bringing to life. You can trust your reader as the co-creator of this entity. Work hard. Make your language and structure ever more precise until what doesn't make sense means exactly what it needs to mean.

(THE CURE FOR) FICTION DEFICIENCY SYNDROME

I've been reading stories from the Golden Age of Science Fiction, most recently "Tunesmith" by Lloyd Biggle, Jr., and it is like being hooked up to an IV.

Have you ever been pretty dehydrated and then gotten an IV? A few hours after I gave birth to my first child, I passed out. The doctors said I was dehydrated, and they gave me an IV. I had been feeling perfectly fine: tired, sure, and maybe a little thirsty. But after they pumped a liter of saline solution into my body, I realized that what I had judged as "fine" was actually pretty bad. Like, wrung-out rag, crawling through the desert bad. But I hadn't noticed. That's what fiction deficiency syndrome is like.

You know what else it's like? It's like being locked in a windowless room by yourself for days or weeks, and it feels perfectly normal. But then when you start reading fiction again, it's like suddenly a good friend shows up, and they bring a picnic and take you out in the sun. You spread a blanket under the trees and talk and eat, and maybe a couple of other friends show up, and their kids play in the background, and you lean against somebody's chest and breathe in the sweet air, and you realize that *this* is what life is, not the windowless room.

So here I am, lying under the trees with Lloyd Biggle, Jr. and Poul Anderson ("Call Me Joe"), and I can see Theodore Sturgeon walking toward us and waving, because I have an anthology.[*]

There's plenty of room on this blanket, and we've still got almost a gallon of lemonade.

Why don't you come join us?

---

[*] *Masterpieces: The Best Science Fiction of the Century* edited by Orson Scott Card.

ACCEPT THE MAGIC OF IMAGINATION

When I was a kid at Saint Lucy's Catholic Church, the altar boys used to ring a little golden bell when the priest raised the host. I watched from my wooden pew and wondered if that was the moment when the miracle happened, when the host changed from bread to the body of Christ. Because otherwise why did they ring the bell?

They don't ring it anymore. I know they used to because my ears still vibrate with its sound, but actually I had forgotten the bell until I went to a poetry reading. The poet described his experience as an altar boy waiting for the time to ring the bell.* The other altar boy, his rival, could ring the bell so beautifully that you knew it worked, that the bread always transformed. The action of the poem happens when it's the boy's turn to ring, and you experience with him the buildup of anxiety as the priest

---

* I wish I could remember who the poet was or what the poem was called. If this sounds like a poem you wrote, please let me know so I can give you credit.

raises the host, up, up, and finally at the apex he has to ring the bell, and it doesn't make the magic sound but instead goes all wonky and wobbly. The poet gave a brilliant performance, and you really believed that he was the altar boy trying to ring the bell to transform the bread into body and failing, failing, failing, just like we all think we fail at the things we care about most.

Maybe that's why the Church stopped ringing the bell, because it makes people believe that something humans do is what's changing the host, and the whole point is that it's not what we do: that the ritual is not the magic, that God is the magic.

Now maybe you don't believe in any god, or you don't believe in the Catholic God, but please still listen to me because I'm not trying to convert you, I'm just making an analogy.

The Ritual Is Not the Magic

Rituals can help you with your writing. For example, Isabelle Allende uses the ritual of lighting a small candle and writing until it burns out.[*]

But the ritual is not the magic. The ritual is a container for the magic: it may be necessary, but it is not sufficient, and there are many rituals and practices that can work.

---

[*] Allende said this during a Q&A I attended at Bookshop Santa Cruz, in Santa Cruz, California.

The magic comes from somewhere else—I call it the Place. You can't control the magic; you can only invite it. You can only make your house ready for it. And then you have to step back and accept that you've done your part. You have to relax and let the guest come in. At church, we hold up the bread, we ring the bell. But the miracle happens through no action of our own. The miracle comes from God, comes by grace, whether we deserve it or not.

The miracle of imagination is the same.

The Gift

Try this improv exercise, adapted from Patricia Ryan Madson.* Go ahead and actually do this. It only takes a minute.

Imagine a closed box, a gift for you.

Let yourself accept the box that has already popped into your mind. Let yourself notice its details: its size, its shape. Is it wrapped? Does it have a ribbon? Hold the box in your hands and feel its weight.

Now imagine yourself opening the box. Let yourself find the gift inside.

What did you find? It's yours to keep and use. I wish you the joy of it.

---

* *Improv Wisdom: Don't Prepare, Just Show Up* by Patricia Ryan Madson.

Accept the Gift

Who puts the gift in the box? Not you. The gift comes from the Place. When you're writing, remember this: you don't have to "make it up." You only have to accept what's in the box and write it down. Sometimes you might want to refuse it, saying, "I don't know what's in there," or "I can't think of anything," but try not to be afraid. Remember that you don't make the gift.

Steven Pressfield, author of *The War of Art*, says that his religion is this: that no matter how many times you open the box, there's always something inside.

We are surrounded and interpenetrated by love and support, always. You think you breathe all by yourself? No. The atmosphere breathes you: it's the pressure of the air outside that pushes air into your lungs. Our own agency is nothing compared to the forces that continually support and help us.

Imagination is not ourselves. The gift comes from the Place. All you have to do is accept it.

When you're writing, you don't have to "make it up." You only have to accept what's in the box and write it down.

"I WANT THESE BUT DON'T KNOW HOW"

What do you do with the pieces you don't yet have the skill to finish?

I used to leave them around in notebooks and never finish them. Half-abandoned, half-forgotten, they were a source of nebulous anxiety, because I vaguely planned to get back to them someday. Sometimes I'd remember one and think, "Hey, I know what to do with that now!" but usually I wouldn't be able to find it.

After I started believing in myself* enough to organize my writing, I developed a way to give those pieces a better chance at life. All it requires is a place to store the pieces you still want to finish.

I mostly write short pieces, and I have a fairly complex system that helps me finish and publish them, but what I'm talking about today only requires a single folder, either digital or paper.

I call my folder "I want these but don't know how." In it, I keep the pieces I don't yet know how to finish. I only

---

* See "How to Believe in Yourself" on page 105.

put something in there if I want to finish it, and I've tried my best, but I just can't figure out how to make it work. I know it is safe in my special folder, so I can forget about it for now and concentrate on something I actually have the skill to finish, knowing that I am improving my skills all the time and can come back to the piece whenever I want.

The folder is right in the middle of my workspace, so every now and then, often when I'm procrastinating writing something else, I look into it and read through some of the pieces, and every now and then I discover that I do know how to finish one of them. Or sometimes I've recently learned a new structure or technique I can try on one of them, and I try it. Maybe I still don't know how to finish the piece, but I learn a lot. Sometimes what I learn helps me finish a different piece.

This folder is also important for its symbolic meaning. By using this folder, I declare, "These pieces I've started are important to me, and I give them space in my life." By using this folder I accept that I want something, even though I don't know how to get it yet. By using this folder I take my work seriously, I act as though I believe in myself, and I thereby increase my confidence as a writer.

If you intend to write for your whole life, you need systems that support that intention. If you don't have a place to keep the pieces you don't yet know how to finish, you might try making a special folder where they can live. I'd recommend keeping the entire text of each piece in the folder because it gives you more of a chance to get back into it. If you just have a list, it's harder to idly start reading a piece and suddenly figure out how to finish it.

Your work matters. The pieces you care about deserve to be finished.* I hope this method helps you finish more of them.

P.S. I got the idea for this essay because I just finished a story that used to be in "I want these but don't know how."

---

* See "Please Finish Your Story" on page 24.

If you intend to write for your whole life, you need systems that support that intention.

BORGES LOVES ME?

Can writing a story cause a story to happen? Here's a story about that ...

Once upon a time, I read Jorge Luis Borges's short stories in Spanish and enjoyed them. I loved his ideas, I enjoyed the things he's interested in: infinity, loneliness, time, math. I never noticed him as a writer; I just read the stories for what happened in them—or not even what happened in them: for the ideas they contained.

Then one day—I don't actually know what the *then one day* is, but maybe it's how deeply I fell in love with Julio Cortázar, how he writes like he's making love to you, how his sentences touch you word by word and completely control you for the purpose of beautifully giving you pleasure. It's like following someone who really knows how to dance. He writes with such a feeling of relationship, of someone actively caring about you and masterfully acting to lead you through a vivid and compelling experience, even if that experience is about horrible things. I love Cortázar's ideas, too, his themes: recursion, transformation, human relationships, traffic jams that last a year. But more than for his themes, I read him to follow when he dances, to be made love to by masterful sentences.

So then I go back to Borges, and it's like reading the newspaper. But maybe I see him in there somewhere; maybe he's shy. He hides behind sounding like a reporter.

All this is true, but it's possible that the *then one day* was a book cover. One time when our writing group was meeting at Barnes & Noble, Anthony brought over a book in which someone had collected Borges's writing about writing and published it with a cover that looks like a legal pad with a watercolor sketch, a portrait of a young man with longish hair, one supposes a portrait of Borges.* He's looking at you. He's looking at you like he sees you, like he's interested in you as a person. He's looking at you in a way that Borges has never looked at me from his text. It's possible that this portrait is what made me wish he would.

Whatever the *then one day* was, I started having this annoying unrequited love for Borges. Before, I just read his stories and was interested in their content, and didn't care about him except for as the name on the cover, like a logo that lets you know what sort of story you'll find inside. But now I was reading the stories trying to get him to look at me. Searching for any moment, no matter how tiny, of interest from the person behind the text. Looking for clues, obsessing over phrases, trying to wring attention from a

---

* *On Writing* by Jorge Luis Borges (Penguin Classics).

stone. Of course I failed. Even when he talks about his own unrequited love for Beatriz, he's just a journalist stating facts.* Even when he describes the jealousy that prompts him to destroy his rival, it's like reading a newspaper report that just weirdly happens to be written in the first person. After a while, I sort of stopped reading him. In fact, I stopped reading fiction much at all, especially in Spanish. I don't think these things are related, but you never know.

I'm not a stranger to longing, to unrequited love, to little obsessions, to paying very close attention to the way someone moves, in fiction or in person. Borges wasn't the only object of that kind of attention; I've done this for as long as I can remember. And at some point I felt like I was suffering too much, that it wasn't a good way of life, and I decided to give up longing. Good idea, I said. I don't have to live like that anymore. If people are my friends, then they're my friends, and I will face them straight on and be myself and not allow that ache in my chest to spiral out toward them and touch them with its tendrils, stroking their expressions and movements and wishing for a connection that's like an author meeting your eyes from his text. I won't even allow that ache to exist at all. I'll just be me, standing firm, without apology, the way I've trained myself to do in my writing.

It actually seemed to be working. I missed the feeling of longing, but I was happier. And my relationships were

---

* "The Aleph" (original title "El Aleph").

improving. I hadn't read Borges or even thought about him for a long time.

৯

Then one day (can you have another *then one day*? I guess you can). I found a copy of Borges's complete poetry in, guess where, Barnes & Noble. The store has a large Spanish language section, but most of the books are translations from English: lose 20 pounds in 20 days, chicken soup for the chocolate lover's soul, organize your office. Also, although the employees are wonderful people who are good at organizing books, I'm pretty sure they don't speak Spanish, and the organization is general at best. So, there between *Freakanomics* and an affirmations coloring book, is a one-inch-thick white spine with black serif letters: Borges *Poesía Completa*.

I pull it out. Finding actual Spanish-language literature in this section is an unexpected delight. And the cover of this book is completely designed to force me to buy it. Thick creamy paper with some kind of texture, coated but not shiny, with that same serif font in large letters at top and bottom; and in the center, floating as if in a universe of pure ideas, a photograph of a piece of paper art, a three-dimensional marvel that twists and folds back on itself like one of Borges's stories.

I'm supposedly shopping for Christmas presents, but I have to have this book. I didn't know Borges even wrote poetry, except for that one that gets passed around the internet, the one where the speaker wishes he'd eaten more ice cream and fewer fava beans (in the English version it's lima beans), the one that Borges totally didn't write, never in a million years, but maybe someone who wished he'd look at her wrote it and attributed it to him and sent it around the internet so that she could pretend that at the end of his life he regretted never loving her in words and wrote this poem to say sorry. Well, I'm not a fan of that poem, and I'm sure he never wrote it, even if he felt that way, so I'm willing to give his poetry a chance. I pretend to rationalize my decision, but really I just buy the book.

And I promise myself I'll read it without longing, and that I won't let any longing seep back into the rest of my life either.

Mostly I succeed, although I do keep an eye out for him to seem human. If there's anywhere you could drop the reporter's voice, it's in poetry. Of course poems can be hard to understand, especially when they're not in your native language, and in spite of passing as a native speaker in daily life, I still have a relatively limited Spanish vocabulary, mostly due to not reading enough. But I read a few, and I try to understand them, and I don't really connect with any, but they're not bad. And then life gets busy and the book sits on the shelf with its beautiful cover, and I look at the cover sometimes and wonder when I might read it again, but that's all.

I'm seeing the power of writing a story to cause a story to happen.

After a while I get invited to do a reading for a multilingual poetry night, and I plan to read Neruda, but when I go and look at the poems I have partly memorized, they are too difficult and long, and I don't have time to even figure out what they mean, let alone prepare to present them to an audience. So I pick up Borges's book.

I open it randomly. I know before I even look at the page that this poem will be the one I read at the event, that it will be good, that it will stay with me for my whole life. Its title in English would be "Manuscript found in a book by Joseph Conrad."* It rhymes in such a beautiful way, it's the perfect poem for this event, since most of the people there will not understand Spanish. I try to memorize it, and I get pretty far but not far enough, but I do look up all the words in the dictionary and come to a pretty good understanding of it. And when I read it at the event, I understand it even more, and in the last stanza I let my walls drop, and I put all my months and years of suppressed longing into my performance, and when I'm done I feel like the longing is in the text. I can't tell if it was there before or not.

I don't know if I've finally seen Borges, if he's actually let me in, but something has changed. Since I structured this as a story, it would be great if this could be the happy ending: through this poem, I've finally connected with

---

* Original title: *"Manuscrito hallado en un libro de Joseph Conrad."*

Borges. I don't feel it in the moment; I can only tell that something has changed in my relationship to the poem. But writing this as a story is changing me too. That ending fits the narrative, so I'm starting to think that it's real. I'm hoping it will be real. I'm seeing the power of writing a story to cause a story to happen.

I reread the poem. I try not to jump to conclusions or even read ahead. I attend to my experience.

The sound of this poem embraces me: its cadence, its rhymes. I feel the poem's voice: its inflections, its emotions. I still haven't looked Borges in the eye, he still has never looked at me. But he has spoken to me, and I have listened with my whole body. Maybe he isn't visual. Maybe he reaches out through sound. I still want to look into his eyes, but I've been in love with people through their voice before. Maybe this will be enough.

It is enough to make me read another poem.

When somebody tells you to take something out, sometimes the solution is to do it more.

DO IT MORE

When somebody tells you to take something out, sometimes the solution is to do it more. This often works in visual art: that area of purple in the upper right corner of your painting, the one that's "ruining" the composition? Instead of removing it, put more purple in other parts of the painting. Suddenly it all comes together.

I think this applies to many writing situations as well. For example, I'm editing a story right now where the first-person narrator uses a few puns and plays on words.[*] I've worked with this author before, and I know she loves this sort of thing, but for some reason I wanted to tell her to take out one of the puns. Then I noticed that the ending of the story hinges on a pun as well. Okay, I admit that I had originally wanted to change the ending, too. But I'm oversensitive to puns because I usually remove them from my own writing. This narrator could keep these two puns,

---

[*] "Wild Hair" by Ruth Littmann-Ashkenazi. You can find it as an instant book at *www.thinkinginkpress.com/instant-books/*

but in order for them to work, she probably needs to have more. At least one more, toward the beginning, to establish this habit in her voice and character, and set us up to accept the ending.

Of course, this sort of free-floating advice must be applied carefully, because nothing works in every situation. I'll see how I feel after the story is done. But I think it's worth trying out.

What about you? Do you have a piece where some element seems out of place? Maybe a character, a certain way of talking, a scene? Why not try adding more and see what happens.

COMING OUT ABOUT OBSESSION

I am obsessed with the stories of Sherlock Holmes. You probably already knew that, so why do I feel the need to come out about it? (I say "come out," because this feels similar to my experience having a nonassumed sexual orientation.)

A colleague recently wrote that she was rereading Sir Arthur Conan Doyle's "The Adventure of the Six Napoleons" in preparation for watching Series 4 of *Sherlock*. There were so many tips of icebergs packed into what she said that I wished I could be as forthcoming about my ideas as she was. But she also said, "Yes, I am just that dorky." I recognized that behavior, the gesture of it, the way I drop my eyes and do a little laugh when I say anything related to Holmes. I realized that I am embarrassed about my obsession.

Why? Am I afraid of the depth of it? I do sense fear there. But when I'm all by myself, I experience only the joy and interest of my obsession. The fear is not of the obsession itself, but rather of its potential social consequences: will people reject me if they find out?

Considering further, I realize that everyone already knows. I write essays titled "Watson Loves Me."* I watch *Sherlock* over and over. I listen to audio recordings of Conan Doyle stories to combat insomnia. The people I care about know these things, and they still like me.

Yeah, says the voice inside, *but they don't know the white-hot obsession, they don't know just how many clock cycles you spend on this, how deep into the water you go.*

But you know what? Maybe they do. Lots of people are fans of things, so maybe they're obsessed with those things the way I am obsessed with the Sherlock Holmes stories. Maybe some of them even incorporate Holmes and Watson into their personal mythology as much as I do. *Hm*, I think, *maybe not*, but that's the fear again.

I have written here about my obsessions, with Holmes, with *Star Trek*, and I faced my audience straight on. It was scary, but I stood tall and told the truth without chickening out. That's because I was writing, and I've spent many years learning not to hide my true self when I write.

I wonder what would happen if I did that in real life, too. I think I might become "more powerful than [I] can possibly imagine."**

---

* See "Watson Loves Me" on page 45.

** In *Star Wars: Episode IV—A New Hope*, Obi-Wan Kenobi says, "If you strike me down, I shall become more powerful than you can possibly imagine." Incidentally, I am not obsessed with *Star Wars*. But lots of people are!

ONLY *ENTERPRISE*

In a previous essay, I said that *Star Trek* is not real.* I think this can cause a lot of misunderstandings, like the title *I Am Not Spock*.**

The truth is that the starship *Enterprise* not only exists, it is more real than real life. More real than an aching shoulder or dinner having to be put on the table. Because those are just facts, and the *Enterprise* is a story.

The experiences of real life are not what feel most real to us. It's the *story* of real life that's real: the meaning we make of it. Even if life is inherently meaningless, as humans we cannot accept that. We insist that it has meaning, and therefore it does—because we make it into a story.

---

* See "No *Enterprise*" on page 101.
** Leonard Nimoy, who played Spock on *Star Trek: The Original Series*, upset many *Star Trek* fans in 1975 when he published an autobiography titled *I Am Not Spock*. In 1995, Nimoy published another autobiography titled *I Am Spock*.

Your writing matters. Your life matters. Your stories matter.

At my writing group, we feel that each other's characters are real, but that's not enough for us: we want these characters to be real to everyone. And the way for that to happen is for people to read those stories, which means publication. This phenomenon is widespread for nonfictional humans too: we want people to understand our stories. To be part of a story makes us real.

There is a memorial on Bainbridge Island for the Japanese-American internment of World War II, which was first implemented there.* The memorial has stories about the families, their own words about what their life was like before and after the internment, even a before-and-after photograph pair: the graduating high school class of the year before the internment, and a photo of the year after, with all the Japanese-American faces missing. Humans make things like this. Humans won't let stories go untold. Humans insist upon healing, upon memorializing, upon speaking out. Humans insist upon meaning. For us, only stories matter. For us, there is only *Enterprise*.

That is the purpose of fiction, of literature, of art: to illuminate what may not be true but which we nevertheless know in our hearts to be true—that the world has meaning beyond itself. Fiction (literature, art), by being an experience with meaning, insists that reality is also meaningful.

---

* The Bainbridge Island Japanese American Exclusion Memorial, in Washington State.

That is the very core of what my life is about, the inner jewel of what I believe: life has meaning beyond itself. Life is as meaningful as a story, if only we could see it.

Your writing matters. Your life matters. Your stories matter.

There is only *Enterprise*.

BE BRAVE AND WRITE

Write to the End* member Jan Petrucha died while I was working on this book. Think of all the things she'll never write. She was a child in London during World War II. Think of the memories that are forever lost now. But she did write down many of them during our sessions at Write to the End.

Sometimes I get discouraged, and I wonder if I am wasting my life, if I'm writing the right things, if any of this will ever matter.

I think about what my writing group members would say, and I think Anthony would tell me to write fiction, to write anything, write, Keiko, write Keiko, write and do not waste time.** That's the real truth of it: pretty soon I'll be

---

* My writing group Write to the End is described in "We Welcome All Writing" on page 14.

** A reference to a line I quoted in the writing prompts at Write to the End, from Annie Dillard's *The Writing Life*: "After Michelangelo died, someone found in his studio a piece of paper on which he had written a note to his apprentice, in the

gone, like Jan, and whatever I haven't published will be unpublished, and whatever I haven't written will be lost forever. The moral of the story is just write, try to get out as much as you can, teach, make art, do anything, try to reach out and let other people know they're not alone. That's all any of us can do: make what's in us to make and try not to dwell on the doubt, the heartache, the wishing you could read the story of your life instead of live it.

For Jan, I will do that. Because she loved me and was never afraid to show it; because she answered the call to create as bravely as anyone I know.

Jan wrote an essay at Write to the End one time. Its title is "Be Brave and Write."* It also could have been titled "Be Brave and Live." Let's keep doing both, together.

---

handwriting of his old age: 'Draw, Antonio, draw, Antonio, draw and do not waste time.'"

* *www.WriteToTheEnd.com/2014/07/jan/be-brave-and-write/*

NOT THE END

Dear writer,

Usually books of advice end with a note of encouragement, written from a place of power and security, from the master teacher who has overcome all the problems the book addresses and promises that you will, too, if you just follow their method. As though in the last chapter they take off the training wheels, and now you're supposed to ride the bike on your own. But if you've been writing for a while, you know that's not true. Nobody overcomes these problems forever. We just get better at solving them sooner. And if you're like me, the training wheels analogy just doesn't apply: we always need other people. I never stop reading books about writing.

While I was working on this book, I fell into funks and had to use the tools I talk about here to get out of them. But sometimes I forgot, and I just felt bad and wasted time. And other times I used someone else's book to help me get going again. Or a writing friend would say something that inspired me to get back to work.

You'll never be done learning, and you can't do everything on your own. We need other people. We need community, both in person and in text. If I've helped you in these pages, if you've enjoyed spending time with me-in-text, come back and visit anytime. You don't have to read from the beginning. You can open the book anywhere, and I'll try to give you what you need in that moment. Keiko-the-book is always constant and loyal, unconditionally there for you.

Keiko-the-human is less reliable, but I try my best. You can connect with Keiko-the-human by joining my mailing list at KeikoOLeary.com. I'd love to hear from you.

Let's keep learning and supporting each other. Let's keep writing. This is not the end.

Your friend,

Keiko O'Leary

RECOMMENDED READING

Here are the books about writing that I mentioned in this book, plus a few extra. If you'd like more details about each of these books and why I recommend them, you can get an expanded version of this list at *www.KeikoOLeary.com/writing-resources*

Change Your Paradigm about Creativity

Impro: Improvisation and the Theatre by Keith Johnstone

The Talent Code: Greatness Isn't Born. It's Grown. Here's How. by Daniel Coyle

Think Deeply about Language and Literature

On Writing by Jorge Luis Borges (Penguin Classics)

1984 by George Orwell

Get Unstuck

Get It Done: From Procrastination to Creative Genius in 15 Minutes a Day by Sam Bennett

The War of Art: Break Through the Blocks and Win Your Inner Creative Battles by Steven Pressfield

Improv Wisdom: Don't Prepare, Just Show Up by Patricia Ryan Madson

Go Deeper with Writing Practice

Writing Down the Bones: Freeing the Writer Within by Natalie Goldberg

Wild Mind: Living the Writer's Life by Natalie Goldberg

Change Your Habits

Switch: How to Change Things When Change Is Hard by Chip Heath and Dan Heath

Empower Yourself in Your Writing Choices

The Sense of Style: The Thinking Person's Guide to Writing in the 21st Century by Steven Pinker

Craft in the Real World by Matthew Salesses

Live as a Writer

Making a Literary Life: Advice for Writers and Other Dreamers by Carolyn See

Bird by Bird: Some Instructions on Writing and Life by Anne Lamott

Be Inspired

Because by Mo Willems and Amber Ren (picture book)

ACKNOWLEDGEMENTS

Thank you, thank you, thank you to the following people and groups:

Write to the End, my beloved writing group: You were the first readers of these essays. Your friendship and encouragement keep me writing.

Thinking Ink Press: Once upon a time at a Write to the End meeting, I said, "If we ever have a small press," and Anthony said, "What do you mean *if?*" I love making books with all of you. Betsy, this book never would have been published without you—not only because of your project management superpowers, but also because your belief in me helps me believe in myself. Liza Olmsted, I love working with an editor, and I love that it's you. Let's keep making things together. Anthony Francis: write, Anthony, write, Anthony, write and do not waste time. I feel blessed to live in the world of literature with you.

Caroline Sanney: My only requirement was that the cover had to "look like a book" but you gave me the cover of my dreams.

Julia Macek: Your art makes me feel like I can fly. Thank you for creating that feeling for my book cover. I'm thrilled every time I see it.

Marilyn Horn: When Liza and I were reviewing your copy edits, we felt like you had saved our lives—multiple times.

Ligaya Yrastorza: Without your physical therapy help, I wouldn't have been able to sit long enough or type long enough to create this book.

Everyone who bought "You have a story to tell" tote bags: This book exists thanks to you.

Amanda Williamsen: Thank you for being a friend in literature and in life, and for bringing me back to poetry after many years away. And thank you for taking me to the Bainbridge Island Japanese American Exclusion Memorial.

Michael Duffy: Even though we just got back into contact after 20 years, I realize you've been with me the whole time. Our friendship is a touchstone for my identity as a writer.

Cheryl Racanelli and Barbara Jacksha, the Prosperous Poets: Our Monday meetings are the magical center of my week. Barb, your game board mediations have helped me bring this book to completion. Cheryl, our weekday Writing Mass has given me peace of mind. And I can never thank you enough for the miracle of reading fiction again, which I attribute to your shed+create class.

Jessica Gatewood, Sinéad Delaney, and Cheryl Ritson, my fellow literary moms: Our talks about books inspire me to keep writing.

Caelyn Dyer: Your courage to be your true self in your writing and life gave me courage to be my true self in this book.

Julie Fast: Your love for this book touched my heart. And we have so much fun together!

Lorraine Haataia, founder of Prolific Writers Life: Thank you for your unwavering support of my work. You are a light for all writers.

Prolific Writers Life: I could not have made this book without Words Count writing sessions. To anyone reading this, if you want a writing community full of experts that will support you, encourage you, and write with you, you'll find it at *www.ProlificWriters.life*

Cristina DeRuiter, my high school Spanish teacher: You gave me the gift of Borges, Neruda, Cortázar, Juan Luis Guerra, Silvio Rodríguez. In spite of all the wonderful literature I've experienced in English, I wouldn't be myself without the literature I love in Spanish.

Bonnie Salera, my high school English teacher: You showed me by example that what I felt inside for literature was okay.

Sam Bennett and community: Sam, your transformational lessons on visibility and productivity, not to mention the compliments list, have changed me into someone who can stand to publish a book. And to all the wonderful people I've met through Sam's programs, your camaraderie has changed me, too.

Meridian University and community: You helped forge my perspective and practices for writing and cultivating writers. Cohort 11, you each hold a section of the hair I cut when I committed to this path. I feel your love always.

Robin Colucci and community: Robin, you say "with a nice subtitle" the way food connoisseurs say "with a nice cabernet sauvignon." Thank you for believing in me, and thank you for all the advice you gave me for this book. And to everyone I've met in Robin's circle, thank you for your enthusiasm and support.

Everyone I've met through local writing organizations: Every time a writer writes or shares their work, it makes more space for other writers to be true to their own work. You've all made space for me.

The students of Room 27: Working with you as writers inspired me to keep going on this book.

My family: Mom, you always turned on the light when I'd been reading so long the sun had gone down. Dad, I learn poems by heart because of you. Thank you for introducing me to e.e. cummings and all the literature we've shared over the years, from "Kubla Khan" to John Prine. Alanna, my sister, I don't understand my life without you. Sergio, my life partner, I love being married with you. Thank you for making space in our lives for this project. Cristina, I find joy in our conversations about literature and art, including superhero movies and Scrooge McDuck. Takeshi, I love making comics and telling collaborative stories with you.

A mi familia chilena: gracias por siempre apoyarme como escritora, aunque muchas veces no hay traducción para que lean lo que escribo.[*]

There are so many more people who influenced my thinking and helped my writing. Even if you're not mentioned here, I appreciate you. Thank you.

---

[*] To my Chilean family: Thank you for always supporting me as a writer, even though there's usually not a version in Spanish for you to read.

ABOUT THINKING INK PRESS

Thinking Ink Press was founded in 2014 in the San Francisco Bay Area by five authors with a love for the printed word. We publish well-crafted and innovative works, including traditional books, limited edition small-format books, and literary postcards. We currently focus on children's health, writing inspiration, queer science fiction and fantasy, flash fiction, poetry, short story collections, and anthologies.

You can find our books and other offerings at *www.ThinkingInkPress.com*. Reach out to us at *contact@thinkinginkpress.com*.

Additional writing resources, as well as a writing tote bag, are available at *www.ThinkingInkPress.com/writing*. With lettering by our own Keiko O'Leary, "You have a story to tell" tote bags are beautiful, functional, and remind you that your writing matters.

www.ingramcontent.com/pod-product-compliance
Lightning Source LLC
Chambersburg PA
CBHW030330100526
44592CB00010B/647